Soccer
Practice Plans
for
Effective Training

Kenneth J. Sherry

Library of Congress Cataloging - in - Publication Data

by, Sherry, Kenneth James
  Soccer Practice Plans for Effective Training

ISBN # 1-890946-56-7
Library of Congress Catalog Number 00-109461
Copyright © October 2000

First edition published 1998 by Admarks,
Beethoven Strasse 12, 82319 Starnberg, Germany.

Art Direction/Layout
Kimberly N. Bender

Illustrations
Karlheinz Grindler

Editing and Proofing
Bryan R. Beaver

Printed by
DATA REPRODUCTIONS
Auburn, Michigan

Cover Photography
EMPICS

REEDSWAIN Publishing
612 Pughtown Road
Spring City • Pennsylvania 19475
1-800-331-5191
www.reedswain.com
EMAIL: info@reedswain.com

Soccer
Practice Plans
for
Effective Training

Kenneth J. Sherry

Published by
REEDSWAIN Publishing

TABLE OF CONTENTS

Section II Further Practices

Section III Small Sided Practices

For many years, usually just before each training session, I wrote a practice plan. This created numerous training logs, some of which are no longer readable because of rain damage, some which were lost in my travels, but believe it or not, some still exist and are extremely useful.

It became apparent to me that I documented the same session several times over in different training logs. So taking the bull by the horns, I decided to put together the most used training sessions into one log book. When writing the log book, I discovered that most of the training layouts were repeated in different sessions, and this made it worth computerizing. This was the birth of this soccer training book, which has helped me plan my practices, without the tedious work of drawing all the layouts time and time again.

The Intended Audience
This coaches' hand book is intended for trainers or coaches who have experience in the basic rudiments of soccer. If you are relatively new to the game or you have never coached a soccer team, then it is advisable to read one of the many soccer books available first. Alternatively, you can participate in a coaching course before using any of these training sessions.

General

The eighty training sessions are subdivided into three main sections:
    Basic Sessions
    Further Sessions
    Small Sided Practices

Each session is a training plan consisting of 2 pages with the right side of the page being the concise training session, and the left side of the page being the description of the training session for use when necessary.

The sizes of the grids and training areas are marked out using cones specified in yards for convenience, although this can be substituted by meters.

Left Side Of Page

Practice Description
This is the description of the practice layout and the general objective of the practice session.

Techniques or Skills
These are the specific techniques or skills required to be coached for this practice, and are a more detailed description of the key factors being used in this practice session.
A technique is the single movement on the ball i.e. a ground pass or heading the ball.
A skill is the application of different techniques and when and where to use them.

Key
This is a quick reference to the individual markings used in the practice layout.

How to Use this Book

Right Side Of Page

Key Factors
The main training points needed for this training session, and should be the ultimate aim of the practice.

Equipment
This is any additional equipment required for a specific practice.

Time
This is the recommended time for the practice session but can be varied depending on the age of the players, the playing conditions such as weather and the number of players available.

Starting Position
In small sided games this suggests where the practice can be started, to create the desired coaching points.

Practice Session Layout
This is a diagram to show where cones should be placed for the practice to be effective, and the parts of the field to be used.

Practice Sequence
This describes how each player should participate in this session and how the different players should interact with each other.

General

This is just a general guideline to warming-up.

Before any training takes place or before a game it is essential that each member of the team warms-up ready for active participation.

Warm-up objectives

To prepare the body to produce the physical response needed during a training session or a game.

To stretch the muscles and tissues to their ideal working length.

To mentally focus on the task at hand, whether it be a training session or a full game.

Warm-up elements

Activities to raise the heart rate to the required level for the task necessary.

Different stretching exercises to gradually stretch the muscles to the working length required.

Activities to produce specific game situations and movements.

Different individual and group ball work.

Warm-up Schedule Before a Game

Whole team warm-up together or in separate units, which should include jogging and stretches for up to ten seconds each.

Team and individual ball work such as running, passing between team members and individual ball juggling.

Speed work such as short sprints and striding sessions.

Individual stretching for full flexibility with each stretch lasting between 20 - 30 seconds.

A team discussion before the game starts with specific instruction to individual players and the team as a whole unit.

Warm-up Schedule Timing and Summary

Team warm-up	5 to 10 minutes
Ball work	5 to 10 minutes
Speed work	5 minutes
Further stretching	5 minutes
Team discussion	5 minutes

Things to watch

Jogging before stretching.

A whole range of stretches, should be used.
First stretches up to 10 seconds.

Do not bounce the stretches just gradually pull the muscle.

The second stretches after running and ball work should be between 20 and 30 seconds.

Do not allow shooting or long passes before the players are stretched out and warmed-up.

Cool Down or warm down

The cool down process is to help the body gradually adjust from exercise to a resting state.

Light jogging and long held stretches after a game or a training practice for up to 10 minutes.

General

The fitness of soccer players has always been brought into question, as the tendency of players is to be lazy and just want to play a game. Although we as coaches would like our players to be able to run for 90 minutes non stop, we must consider that to be able to run for that amount of time would require a player to run continually at one pace, emulating a long distance runner.

First of all, we must consider that a soccer player will have several different phases of activity during a game, such as standing, walking, jogging, running at controlled pace and sprinting. Soccer players do not generally need to be trained in standing and walking as they are very apt in these qualities. The third activity, jogging, although normally part of warming up, warming down and general activity around the training field, should not be avoided and some form of running at one speed is very essential. The last two, running at a controlled pace and sprinting, should be trained in special sessions and whenever possible include a ball.

There should always be a balance between running and recovery, to achieve the required fitness. The number of repetitions and the recovery time between can be varied the more fit the players become.

Three sessions have been included for speed and endurance training:

Shuttle sprinting and dribbling with the ball.

Sprint to be first to the ball and jog for recovery.

Running with the ball and weaving in and out of cones.

Shuttle sprinting and dribbling with the ball
Fitness Aims:
1. Sprint to collect the ball for 30 yards
2. Dribble the ball at controlled speed for 30 yards through the cones
3. Recover while 3 other players perform the task

Session sequence:
Use 4 players for each grid. One player runs to collect a ball "AT FULL SPEED" from the other side of the grid and dribbles the ball back through the cones "AT CONTROLLED SPEED". The next player runs from the opposite side to collect the ball and the practice alternates. Each player runs at least 5 times, but this may depend on age and fitness.

Layout:
Set out 10 cones, 3 yards apart in one line and make enough lines to accommodate the whole team.

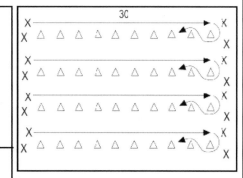

Sprint to be first to the ball and jog for recovery
Fitness Aims:
1. Sprint to collect the ball for 20 yards against an opponent
2. Control the ball and shoot.
3. Jog for recovery while other players perform the task.

Session sequence:
Use 2 players at one time.
Both players run on command to collect the ball from the server. The one who receives the ball first controls the ball and shoots to score a goal.
Both players should make a recovery run around the outside of the cones, and collect the ball, while the next 2 players proceed with the practice.

Layout:
Use a goal and penalty area and place cones around the penalty area.
Place 2 cones each side of the penalty spot 5 yards apart, and 2 cones outside the penalty area, 5 yards from the edge of the penalty area where the players should start their run.

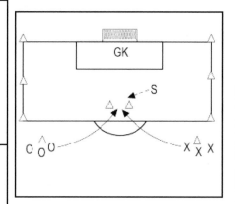

Running with the ball while weaving around cones
Fitness Aims:
1. Sprint to collect the ball for 25 yards
2. Dribble the ball at controlled speed through 5 sets of cones for 50 yards
3. Recover while 3 other players perform the task

Session sequence:
Use 4 players for each grid.
Each player starts by running diagonally across the grid to collect the ball passed by another player.
With the ball the player runs at controlled speed, using the "Running with the ball technique" across the grid and through the cones until reaching the other side of the grid.
Each player takes turns to complete the practice with a minimum of 5 turns.

Layout:
Set out a grid 10 X 25 yards using 2 lines of cones spaced 5 yards apart. Set out enough grids to accommodate the whole team.

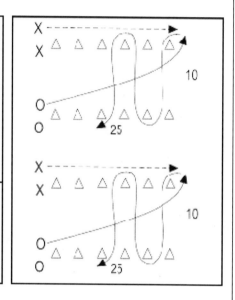

Practice Recommendations

All these fitness sessions allow for continuous movement with and without the ball.

This type of training can be varied in repetitions and recovery time. Always build up the sessions over several weeks with increased repetitions and shorter recovery times.

To increase the fitness, the number of players to a grid should be decreased and the recovery time reduced accordingly. The fitness can also be improved by increasing the number of times each player performs the activity.

To make it more interesting, allow players and teams to compete against each other.

Ground passes

Layout:
This practice can be set up with grids of 3 times 10 X 10 yards. Initially 2 players will use a 10 X 10 yard grid. Depending on the number of players further grids can be laid out.

General:
In the first practice make sure the players are actively moving, not just standing and passing.

In the second practice the moving player X must run from side to side. After 10 times switch the players over.

The third practice requires both players moving but one makes a diagonal pass and the other player makes a square pass. This practice sequence does require thinking to create the correct passing movement. If this sequence does not work at first, return to a starting position and begin again.

Techniques for ground passing

Ground passing:
The foot is turned outward so that the inside of the boot makes contact with the ball at right angles to the line of the pass.

The ankle must be firm to create a hockey stick effect.

To keep the ball low, the contact of the boot on the ball should be through the horizontal mid-line of the ball, with the body over the ball.

The non-kicking foot should be placed alongside the ball far enough away to allow a free-swinging movement of the kicking leg.

The position of the head should be steady with eyes looking down at the ball.

KEY

Ball Movement	◄--------------	Attacking Player	X
Player Movement	◄──────────	Defending Player	0
		Goalkeeper	GK

Key Factors:
1. The kicking foot should strike through the bottom half of the ball.
2. The non-kicking foot should be placed slightly behind the ball.
3. The body should lean slightly back.
4. Head should be steady with the eyes on the ball.

EQUIPMENT: GRIDS CREATED FROM CONES, 10 BALLS

TIME: 30 MIN.

Practice Sequence 1:
10 minutes
2 players pass to each other using lofted passes both trapping and returning the pass.
Both players should use all three techniques as described.

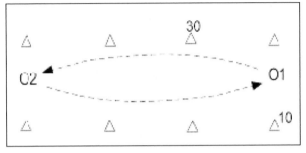

Practice Sequence 1

Practice Sequence 2:
10 minutes
X passes the ball to O1 and the O players make lofted passes to each other, while X moves inside the middle grid threatening the passes.
Both players should use all three techniques as described.

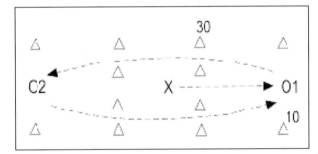

Practice Sequence 2

Practice Sequence 3:
10 minutes
X1 passes the ball to O1 and the O players make lofted passes to each other, while the X players move inside the middle grid threatening the passes.
Both of the O players should use all three techniques as described.

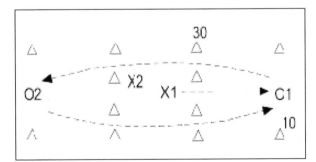

Practice Sequence 3

Trapping the ball

Layout:
Set up this practice with a grid of 4 times 10X10 yards depending on the numbers of players to be trained. Use this grid set up for all 4 practice sequences.

General:
The throw from the O player should be a good standard throw-in.

Switch the players after 10 traps of the ball.

Each practice sequence requires the same procedure with a different trapping technique.

Techniques for trapping the ball

Trapping with the foot:
Keep the foot at right angles to the ball with the body over the ball, allowing the foot to swing back as the foot contacts the ball to cushion the impact of the ball.

Trapping with the knee:
Keep the knee and thigh at right angles to the ball, allowing the leg to move down on contact to cushion the impact of the ball.

Trapping with the chest:
Keep the chest at right angles to the ball, allowing the surface of the chest to withdraw on impact with the ball.

General:
The position of the head should be steady with eyes looking at the ball.

KEY

Ball Movement	◄ - - - - - - - - -	Attacking Player	X
Player Movement	◄─────────	Defending Player	0
		Goalkeeper	GK

Key Factors:
1. Keep the body square to the ball.
2. Cushion the impact of the ball.
3. Use the specific part of the body to trap the ball.
4. Head steady with eyes on the ball.

EQUIPMENT: GRIDS CREATED FROM CONES, 10 BALLS

TIME: 20 MIN.

Practice Sequence 1:
5 minutes
0 throws the ball to X who traps the ball with the foot and passes it back.

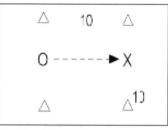

Practice Sequence 1

Practice Sequence 2:
5 minutes
0 throws the ball to X who traps the ball with the knee and passes it back.

Practice Sequence 3:
5 minutes
0 throws the ball to X who traps the ball with the chest and passes it back.

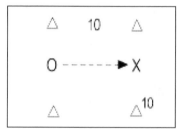

Practice Sequence 2

Practice Sequence 4:
5 minutes
0 throws the ball to X who traps the ball with the chest then drops the ball to the knee and ends up with a trap at the feet.
X should end up passing the ball back.

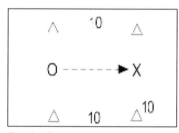

Practice Sequence 3

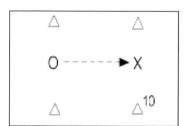

Practice Sequence 4

Dribbling

Layout:
For the first practice set up grids of 10 X 10 yards and, if there are extra play-ers add an additional grid of 10 X 10 yards.

For the second and third practices create grids of 30 X 10 yards with a goal created from cones, but only 3 to 4 yards apart at one end.

General:
In practice 1, 4 to 5 players try to dribble around the grid and where possi-ble kick an opponent's ball out of the grid without losing control of their own ball. The coach should use commands, in order to convey to the players when to change direction, and when to stop and start.

In practice 2 use 4 players in each grid and switch out players.

In practice 3 use all 4 players and create a 2 v 2 situation.

Techniques for dribbling

Dribbling the ball:
The dribbling player should approach moving straight towards the oppo-nent at a controlled speed, keeping close control of the ball.

The dribbling player should unbalance the opponent by changing direction and or pace outside of the tackling distance. Combining a feint with a change in direction can unbalance an opponent.

After unbalancing the opponent, the dribbling player should explode into space behind the opponent.

KEY

Ball Movement	⟶		Player Movement	------→
Attacking Player	X		Defending Player	0
Server	S		Goalkeeper	GK

Key Factors:
1. Close control of the ball.
2. Run straight at the opponent.
3. Slow in/fast out.
4. Fake out opponent.

EQUIPMENT: GRIDS CREATED FROM CONES, 10 BALLS

TIME: 30 MIN.

Practice Sequence 1:
10 minutes
5 Players dribble a ball inside the grid, turning first with the inside of the foot then with the outside of the foot.
Each player must keep control of the ball without touching other players

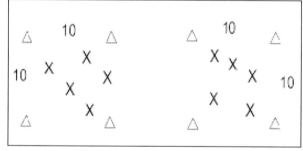

Practice Sequence 1

Practice Sequence 2:
10 minutes
Server S passes the ball to X who attempts to dribble past O to the small goal at the other end.

Practice Sequence 3:
10 minutes
Server X2 passes the ball to X1 who attempts to dribble past O1 and O2 to the small goal at the other end. Both X1 and X2 play against O1 and O2.

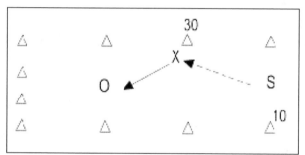

Practice Sequence 2

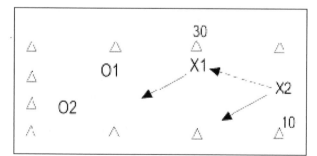

Practice Sequence 3

Ball control while running

Layout:
This practice can be made up of several grids of 10 X 30 yards to accommodate the whole team.

General:
The players should always be running during their time in the middle and execute the technique properly.

Keep the practicing player limited to 10 times and then change to the next player.

In practice 1 the players can use 2 touch (control and pass back).

In practice 2 the player should trap the ball with the chest and pass the ball back.

In practice 3 the ball should be headed directly back to the server.

Techniques for controlling the ball

Trapping with the foot:
Keep the foot at right angles to the ball with the body over the ball, allowing the foot to swing back as the foot makes contact with the ball to cushion the impact.

Trapping with the chest:
Keep the chest at right angles to the ball, allowing the surface of the chest to withdraw on impact with the ball.

Heading the ball:
The ball should be struck with the upper part of the forehead keeping the ball down and the eyes looking at the ball.

Ground passes:
The foot is turned outward so that the inside of the boot makes contact with the ball at right angles to the line of the pass. The ankle must be firm to create a hockey stick effect.

KEY

Ball Movement	→	Player Movement	------>
Attacking Player	X	Defending Player	0
Server	S	Goalkeeper	GK

Key Factors:

1. Body square to the ball.
2. Run at controlled speed.
3. Bring ball under control first time.
4. Head steady with eyes on the ball.

EQUIPMENT: GRIDS CREATED FROM CONES, 10 BALLS   TIME: 30 MIN.

Practice Sequence 1:

10 minutes
X runs between the 2 servers (S) who are making ground passes, makes a foot trap with the ball and returns the ball with a ground pass to the server

Practice Sequence 2:

10 minutes
X runs between the 2 servers (S) who are making throw-ins, and makes a chest trap with the ball and returns the ball with a ground pass to the server.

Practice Sequence 3:

10 minutes
X runs between the 2 servers (S) who are making throw-ins and heads the ball back to the server.

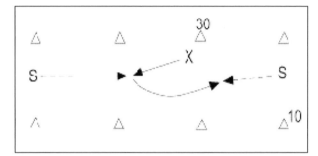

Practice Sequence 1

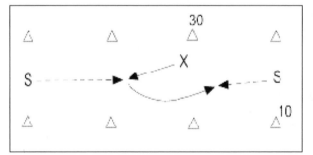

Practice Sequence 2

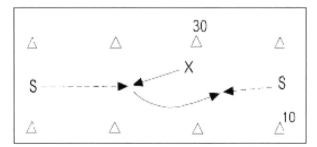

Practice Sequence 3

19

Heading the ball

Layout:
For this practice set up several grids of 10 X 30 yards to accommodate the whole team practice. Create a standard width goal from cones at 8 yards for practice 2 and 3.

General:
Practice 1 is a defensive heading practice.

In practice 2 add a goalkeeper, this can be one of the other players to make it realistic, and mark the exact goal area with cones. This time the player heads the ball down into the goal.

In practice 3 have 2 players, one as a defender and the other as an attacker, and keep the goalkeeper.

In all the practices limit the number of times each player heads the ball to 10 before changing.

Techniques for heading the ball

Heading in defense:
Keep the eyes on the ball and strike the ball with the upper part of the forehead.

Head the ball up and out of the area in the opposite direction to which it came.

Heading in attack:
Keep the eyes on the ball, jumping if necessary to head the ball down with the upper part of the forehead.

KEY

Ball Movement	⟶	Player Movement	------→
Attacking Player	X	Defending Player	0
Server	S	Goalkeeper	GK

Key Factors:
1. Attack the ball.
2. Head the ball with the upper part of the forehead.
3. Body square to the ball.
4. Keep eyes on the ball.

EQUIPMENT: GRIDS CREATED FROM CONES, 10 BALLS, BIBS   **TIME: 30 MIN.**

Practice Sequence 1:
10 minutes
The server makes a throw-in to X who heads the ball up and out of the area.
Switch between servers.

Practice Sequence 2:
10 minutes
The server makes a throw-in to X who heads the ball down into the goal.
Switch between servers.

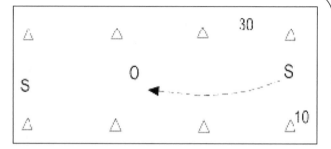

Practice Sequence 1

Practice Sequence 3:
10 minutes
The defender or the attacker must make a header.
The server makes a throw-in to X and O and both should try to head the ball.
Switch between servers.

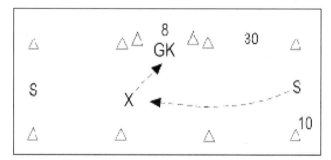

Practice Sequence 2

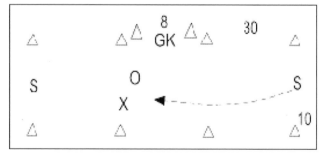

Practice Sequence 3

Basic shooting

Layout:
Use a goal and penalty area with players starting from behind the penalty area.

General:
In practice 1 organize the players on the edge of the penalty area and coach each player to shoot correctly.

In practice 2 create 2 lines of players with one player acting as the server. Each player passes the ball to the server, runs to collect the returned pass and shoots. The player can shoot directly or control the ball first, depending on the player's ability. All players should practice from the right and the left side.

In practice 3 set up the same as practice 2, but this time the server throws the ball in the air for the player to run onto, control and shoot or take a first time shot.

Techniques for basic shooting

Shooting with the instep:
The ankle of the kicking foot should be extended and firm and make contact with the ball through the vertical mid-line of the ball, with the body over the ball.

Shooting with inside of the foot:
The foot should be pointed outward with the ankle firm and extended, with the body over the ball.

General:
The non-kicking foot should be placed alongside the ball far enough away to allow a free-swinging movement of the kicking leg.

The position of the head should be steady with eyes looking down at the ball while shooting.

KEY				
Ball Movement	⟶		Player Movement	----➤
Attacking Player	X		Defending Player	0
Server	S		Goalkeeper	GK

Key Factors:

1. Check the position of the goalkeeper.
2. Accuracy of the shot over power.
3. Head down and steady with the eyes on the ball.
4. Strike middle or top half of the ball.

EQUIPMENT: Goal and penalty area, 10 Balls

TIME: 30 min.

Practice Sequence 1:

10 minutes

The Goalkeeper throws the ball to each player in turn and each player controls the ball and takes a shot on goal.

Practice Sequence 2:

10 minutes

X1 passes the ball to the server who returns the pass.

The ball is played by the server in the path of the running X player who shoots for a goal without controlling the ball first.

Practice Sequence 3:

10 minutes

This is the same set up as practice 2 but this time the server throws the ball in the air in the path of the running X player who controls the ball and shoots.

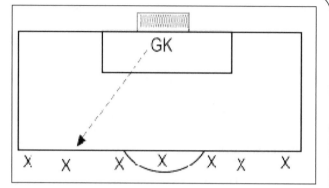

Practice Sequence 1

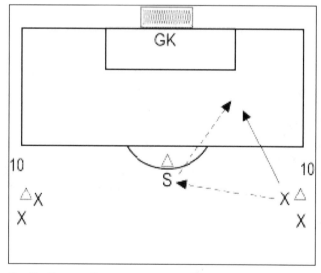

Practice Sequence 2

Shooting across the goal

Layout:
Use the goal and penalty area.
In practice 2 create a funnel at the back post of goal. This is a V shape with the nearest cones 3 yards apart on either side of the back goal post, extending out 10 yards, with the outer cones also being 10 yards apart.

General:
In the first practice the player should play the ball to the server and collect the returned pass for a shot across the goal.

In the second practice the X1 player passes the ball to X2 while O defends against the X players. The X2 player plays the ball to X1 and runs into the funnel to collect the rebound or the misdirected shot. The O player should defend realistically.

Techniques for shooting across the goal

Shooting across the goal:
The player should observe the position of the goalkeeper and aim the shot at the far post.

Concentrate on accuracy and strike through the middle or top half of the ball.

Keep the head down and steady for contact on the ball.

General:
The back of goal is the area that is most dangerous for the defending team. Utilize this funnel area to attack for re-bounds and missed shots.

KEY

Ball Movement	⟶		Player Movement	┄┄┄➤
Attacking Player	X		Defending Player	0
Server	S		Goalkeeper	GK

Key Factors:
1. Check the position of the goalkeeper.
2. Accuracy of the shot to the far post.
3. Head down and steady with the eyes on the ball.
4. Strike middle or top half of the ball.

EQUIPMENT: GOAL AND PENALTY AREA, 10 BALLS, BIBS, CONES

TIME: 30 MIN.

Practice Sequence 1:

15 minutes
The X player passes the ball to the server who returns the pass in the path of the X player.
X collects the pass and controls the ball for a shot across the goal.

Practice Sequence 2:

15 minutes
This is the same set up as practice 1 but the O defender is included in the play to threaten the X players.
This time the X2 player runs into the funnel at the back of the goal after the ball is passed back to X1.

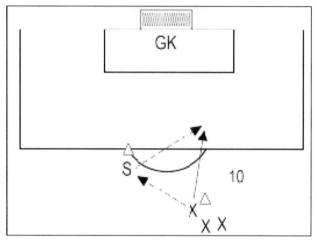

Practice Sequence 1

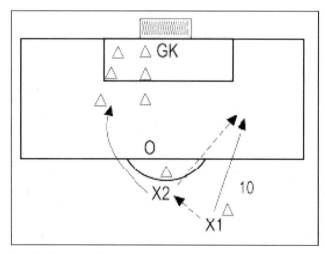

Practice Sequence 2

Defending turning and support

Layout:
Set up the practice with grids 30 X 10 yards with 4 players each.

General:
The starting position should be with the X player at the front of the middle 10 X 10 yard grid and the defender O at the back of the middle 10 X 10 yard grid.

In practice 1 coach the basic defending techniques.

In practice 2 add the second defender and coach defending support techniques.

In practice 3 both defenders should be defending and supporting.

Techniques for defending and supporting

Defending:
The defending player should watch the ball when in a challenging position.

It is important for the defending player to adopt the ideal position which is a little less than one yard from the attacker.

The defender should be patient and concentrate on when to select the correct moment to tackle. The best moment is when the attacker attempts to turn.

Supporting:
The supporting player should be positioned at an angle behind the defender, in line with where the attacker is being steered.

The supporting player should communicate with the defender.

KEY

Ball Movement	⟶	Player Movement	- - - - - -➤
Attacking Player	X	Defending Player	0
Server	S	Goalkeeper	GK

Key Factors:
1. Be patient and watch the ball.
2. Prevent the opponent from turning with the ball.
3. Select the correct moment to tackle.
4. Steer the opponent towards the supporting player or the side line.

EQUIPMENT: GRIDS CREATED FROM CONES, 10 BALLS, BIBS

TIME: 30 MIN.

Practice Sequence 1:

10 minutes
S1 passes to X while O challenges as a defender. X attempts to pass to S2.

Practice Sequence 2:

10 minutes
S1 passes to X while O1 challenges as a defender with support from a second defender (O2). X attempts to move the ball to the end of the grid.

Practice Sequence 3:

10 minutes
X2 passes to X1 while O1 challenges as a defender with support from a second defender (O2). X2 supports X1 as an additional attacker, with the aim to move the ball to the end of the grid.

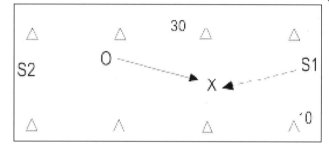

Practice Sequence 1

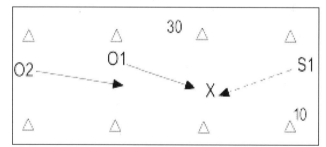

Practice Sequence 2

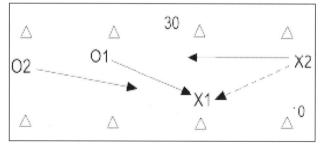

Practice Sequence 3

Defending around the penalty area

Layout:
Use an actual goal and penalty area plus a grid outside the area, which should be the width of the penalty area and 30 yards from the end line .

General:
Start off with an attacker and a defender on each side of the goal.

The goalkeeper should pass to one side and then the other, allowing 1 attacker and 1 defender to practice against each other.

In the second practice allow players from both sides of the goal to be in the play at the same time. This will allow 2 attackers and 2 defenders to practice.

Techniques for defending

Defending:
The defender should close down the space between the attacker quickly and should watch the ball when in a challenging position.

The defending player should adopt the ideal position two to three feet from the attacker.

The defending player should have patience and concentrate on when to select the correct moment to tackle when the attacker attempts to turn.

The supporting player should be positioned at the angle where the attacker is being steered.

KEY

Ball Movement	⟶	Player Movement	----→
Attacking Player	X	Defending Player	0
Server	S	Goalkeeper	GK

Key Factors:
1. Close down the opponent quickly.
2. Prevent opponent from turning.
3. Steer opponent towards the supporting player and or the side line.
4. Supporting player position.

EQUIPMENT: GOAL AND PENALTY AREA, 10 BALLS, BIBS

TIME: 30 MIN.

Practice Sequence 1:
15 minutes
The goalkeeper kicks the ball out to an X player.
The O player defends against the X player.

Practice Sequence 2:
15 minutes
The goalkeeper kicks the ball out to X1 or X2.
O1 and O2 defend against the X players.

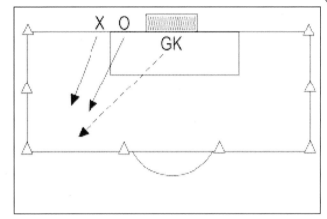

Practice Sequence 1

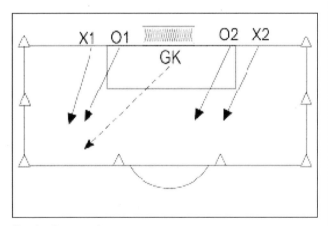

Practice Sequence 2

Tracking and marking players

Layout:
Use an actual goal and penalty area plus a grid outside the area, which should be the width of the penalty area and 30 yards from the end line.

General:
In practice 1 the defender O should track the attacker out of the grid area, but the attacker should attempt to attack the goal.

In practice 2 the two defenders should defend the grid area from the two attackers.

If the ball goes out of the grid, the sequence is finished and the next set of defenders and attackers should start.

Techniques for tracking and marking

Tracking and marking:
The defending player should always keep goal side of the opponent and occupy space.

The defender should always keep the opponent and the ball in view.

The defender should be close enough to challenge the opponent when the ball is passed to the opponent.

The defender should force the opponent to defensive strength or out of the grid area.

KEY

Ball Movement	⟶	Player Movement	----➤
Attacking Player	X	Defending Player	0
Server	S	Goalkeeper	GK

Key Factors:
1. Close opponent down quickly.
2. Keep goal side of the ball.
3. Force opponent across the field.
4. Keep ball and opponent in view.

EQUIPMENT: GOAL AND PENALTY AREA, 10 BALLS, BIBS

TIME: 30 MIN.

Practice Sequence 1:
15 minutes
The server passes the ball to X who dribbles towards the goal.
The O player defends against the X player.

Practice Sequence 2:
15 minutes
The server passes the ball to X1 who dribbles towards the goal with the assistance of attacker X2. O1 and O2 should defend the penalty area, creating a 2 v 2 situation.

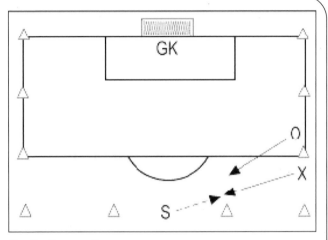

Practice Sequence 1

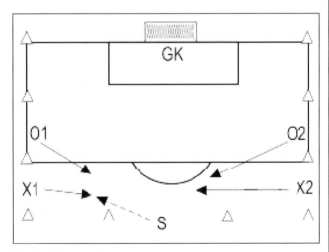

Practice Sequence 2

Creating space as an individual

Layout:
Set up grids 30 X 10 yards with 4 players each

General:
The starting position should be with the X player at the back of the middle 10 X 10 yard grid.

Make sure the defender O marks the attacker X closely.

The practice should be as realistic as possible in the confines of the grid area.

Switch players around to give all players the opportunity to practice.

Techniques for creating space as an individual

Creating space:
The player should draw the opponent out to create space behind the opponent.

The player should move at a controlled speed towards the oncoming ball and change pace quickly when the player decides to receive the ball.

The player can receive the ball face on, therefore having to turn 180 degrees, or at an angle which will allow the player more vision of the space behind the opponent.

The player should receive the ball with the foot furthest away from the opponent and be ready to turn immediately.

KEY

Ball Movement	⟶	Player Movement	- - - - -▶
Attacking Player	X	Defending Player	0
Server	S	Goalkeeper	GK

Key Factors:
1. Move opponent to create space.
2. Move off the opponent with the body at right angles.
3. Receive the ball with the foot furthest away from the opponent.
4. Prepare to turn when receiving the ball.

EQUIPMENT: Grids created from cones, 10 Balls, Bibs   **TIME: 30 min.**

Practice Sequence 1:
10 minutes
S1 passes to X while O challenges as a defender.
X attempts to pass to S2.

Practice Sequence 2:
10 minutes
X2 passes to X1 while O challenges as a defender.
X2 joins X1 as an additional attacker.
The X players attempt to move the ball to the end of the grid.

Practice Sequence 3:
10 minutes
X2 passes to X1 while O1 challenges as a defender with support from a second defender (O2).
X2 supports X1 as an additional attacker with the aim of moving the ball to the end of the grid.

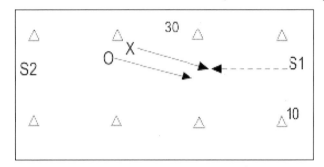

Practice Sequence 1

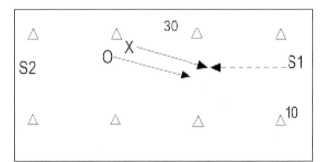

Practice Sequence 2

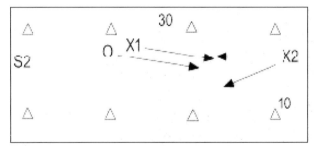

Practice Sequence 3

Running and crossing the ball

Layout:
In practice 1 the grids should be 10 X 30 yards with enough grids to accommodate the whole team.

In practice 2 the target area should be marked so that it can clearly be seen, and should be 20 X 8 yards, extending 2 yards inside the goal area in line with the goal. The running lanes should be at least 10 X 20 yards.

General:
In practice 2 the players should run with the ball and make a cross before leaving the crossing lane.

The cross should be into the target area with a lofted pass.

Techniques for running with ball and crossing

Running with the ball:
Always run at a controlled speed keeping the ball in front, kicking with the outside of the foot.

After each kick lift the head up to survey the situation of when to pass or cross the ball.

Crossing the ball:
The cross should be made with a lofted pass.

KEY				
Ball Movement	———————▶		Player Movement	- - - - - - - - -▶
Attacking Player	X		Defending Player	0
Server	S		Goalkeeper	GK

Key Factors:

1. Run at a controlled speed.
2. Eyes should be on the ball each time the ball is being kicked.
3. Keep head up while running.
4. Cross the ball with a lofted pass into the target area.

EQUIPMENT: Goal and penalty area, 10 Balls, Cones

TIME: 30 min.

Practice Sequence 1:
10 minutes
X runs with the ball until the middle of the last 10 X 10 grid and passes to the next player.
The next X player repeats the process in the opposite direction.

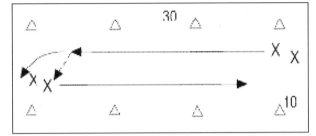

Practice Sequence 1

Practice Sequence 2:
20 minutes
The X players take turns passing the ball to the server, running into the crossing lane and collecting the returned pass.
The X player then runs to the end of the crossing lane and makes a cross into the target area.

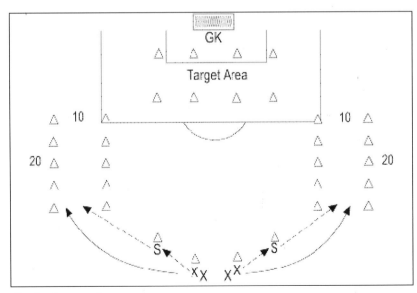

Practice Sequence 2

Goalkeeper ball handling

Layout:
Use an actual goal and a goal area for a realistic practice.

General:
If there are two goalkeepers on the team each can practice with the other, otherwise use one of the field players to assist the coach.

Techniques for goalkeeper ball handling

Stoop technique:
The feet should be placed close enough together to prevent the ball from passing between the legs.

Kneeling technique:
The feet and the lower part of the body should be sideways onto the ball with the knee of the kneeling leg in line with the heel of the other leg.

Waist high technique:
The feet shoulder width apart and the ball collected to the waist.

Chest high technique:
The feet shoulder width apart and the ball collected to the chest.

Head high technique:
The feet shoulder width apart and the ball collected with the hands at head height.

General:
The hands should be behind the ball with palms facing outward.
The ball should be cupped with the hands into the chest after the ball has been collected.
The head should be steady with eyes on the ball as long as possible.

KEY

Ball Movement	⟶		Player Movement	-------⟶
Attacking Player	X		Defending Player	0
Server	S		Goalkeeper	GK

Key Factors:
1. Starting position.
2. Head steady with eyes on the ball.
3. Body square to the ball and palms facing out.
4. Collect the ball and cup it into the chest.

EQUIPMENT: GOAL AND GOAL AREA, 5 BALLS   TIME: 25 MIN.

Practice Sequence 1:
5 minutes- Stoop Technique
The server S kicks the ball to the goalkeeper who collects the ball with a stoop technique.

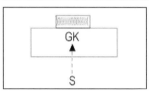

Practice Sequence 1

Practice Sequence 2:
5 minutes- Kneeling Technique
The server S kicks the ball to the goalkeeper who collects the ball with a kneeling technique.

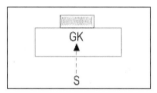

Practice Sequence 2

Practice Sequence 3:
5 minutes- Waist-High Technique
The server S kicks the ball to the goalkeeper who collects the ball from the waist.

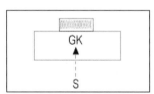

Practice Sequence 3

Practice Sequence 4:
5 minutes- Chest-High Technique
The server S kicks the ball to the goalkeeper who collects the ball from the chest.

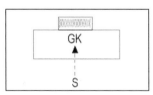

Practice Sequence 4

Practice Sequence 5:
5 minutes- Head-High Technique
The server S kicks the ball to the goalkeeper who collects the ball from head high and brings it down to the chest.

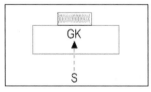

Practice Sequence 5

Goalkeeper moving into line

Layout:
Keep the practice realistic and use an actual goal and penalty area.

General:
Use the field players to move the ball around.

The goalkeeper should move into line with the ball, using a skipping motion.

The goalkeeper should throw the ball out after each shot on goal to one of the field players.

Techniques for the goalkeeper moving into line

Moving into line:
The goalkeeper should use a sideways skipping motion with one foot coming to the other foot, before the first foot is moved again.

The goalkeeper should always be in line with the ball and the cone placed at the middle and rear of the goal.

KEY

Ball Movement	⟶		Player Movement	-------▶
Attacking Player	X		Defending Player	0
Server	S		Goalkeeper	GK

Key Factors:

1. Sideways skipping.
2. Speed of movement.
3. Accuracy of moving into line between the ball and the middle of the goal.
4. Balanced and relaxed.

EQUIPMENT: GOAL AND GOAL AREA, 5 BALLS   TIME: 20 MIN.

Practice Sequence 1:

10 minutes
Servers S1 and S2 take turns at passing the ball to the X player on the opposite side of the penalty area, who runs to collect the ball and dribbles towards the goalkeeper with the intent to score.

Practice Sequence 2:

10 minutes
The X players pass the ball to each other until one X player takes a shot. The goalkeeper stops the ball and throws it back out to one of the players.

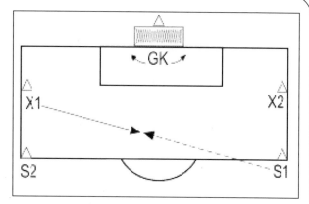

Practice Sequence 1

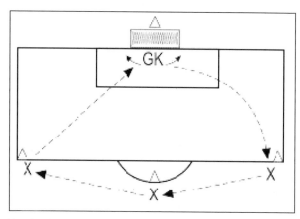

Practice Sequence 2

Throw-ins

Layout:
For practice 1 set up grids of 10 X 10 yards.
For practice 2 and 3 set up grids of 10 X 30 yards.

General:
In the first practice make sure the players are using the correct throw-in techniques.

In the second practice the player must run to receive the throw-in.

In the third practice, while the player runs to receive the throw-in, the defending player should apply pressure.

Techniques for throw-ins

Throwing-in the Ball:

Keep both hands on the ball up to delivery.
Both feet must be on the ground while delivering the throw-in.
The ball must start from behind the head.
Keep the body square with the field and do not turn the body on delivery.
Throw the ball directly to the player receiving the ball or high over defenders.
Keep the head steady while delivering the ball.
Both feet must be behind the touch line or one foot on the touch line.

KEY

Ball Movement	⟶	Player Movement	----→
Attacking Player	X	Defending Player	0
Server	S	Goalkeeper	GK

Key Factors:

1. Throw the ball from behind the head with both hands on the ball.
2. Keep both feet in contact with the ground, perhaps dragging one foot
3. The ball should be thrown to the receiving player at most direct angle
4. Throw the ball hard enough for the receiving player to control the ball.

EQUIPMENT: GRIDS CREATED FROM CONES, 10 BALLS   TIME: 30 MIN.

Practice Sequence 1:
10 minutes
2 players throw the ball in to each other, concentrating on correct throwing action.

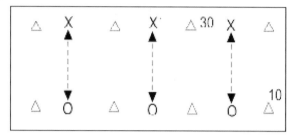

Practice Sequence 1

Practice Sequence 2:
10 minutes
Player O throws the ball to the oncoming player X. The X player starts at a distance of 20 yards and then increases it to 30 yards.

Practice Sequence 3:
10 minutes
X1 throws to the ball to the oncoming player X2.
X2 starts at 20 yards distance while the defender O starts from a distance of 30 yards.
X2 should play the ball back to X1 and start again.
O should pressure X2 to prevent him from receiving the ball.

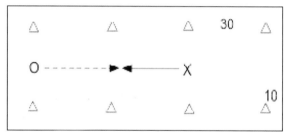

Practice Sequence 2

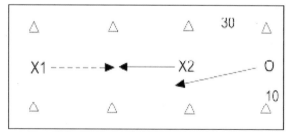

Practice Sequence 3

Dribbling Techniques

Layout:
Set up practice grids of 10 X 10 yards depending on the number of players.

General:
Use the same grids for all three practice sequences.

Techniques for dribbling the ball

The approach:
The approach of the player should commit the opponent by moving straight at the opponent at controlled speed.

Feint and Dummy:
The dribbling player should unbalance the opponent by changing direction and or pace outside of tackling distance. Combining a feint with a change in direction can unbalance an opponent.

Explode into Space:
After unbalancing the opponent the dribbling player should explode into space behind the opponent.

KEY

Ball Movement	⟶	Player Movement	------>
Attacking Player	X	Defending Player	0
Server	S	Goalkeeper	GK

Key Factors:

1. Approach the opponent at controlled speed.
2. Unbalance the opponent just out of tackling distance using one technique.
3. While opponent is unbalanced change direction.
4. Explode into the space behind the opponent

EQUIPMENT: GRIDS CREATED FROM CONES, 10 BALLS   **TIME:** 30 MIN.

Practice Sequence 1:

10 minutes
The X player dribbles using the Matthews move against the defender O.

Techniques of the Matthew's Move:

Move the ball with the inside of the foot and drop the opposite shoulder and then change direction and kick the ball with outside of the same foot and move in the same direction.

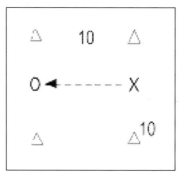

Practice Sequence 1

Practice Sequence 2:

10 minutes
The X player dribbles using the Scissors move against the defender O.

Techniques of the Scissors Move:

Play the ball in front and pretend to play the ball with the outside of the foot but instead step over the ball and play the ball with outside of the opposite foot and move in the same direction.

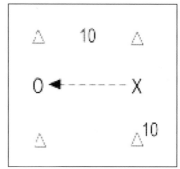

Practice Sequence 2

Practice Sequence 3:

10 minutes
The X player dribbles using the Cruyff Move against the defender O.

Techniques of the Cruyff Move:

Run with the ball directly at the opponent and pretend to shoot but with the same foot drag the ball back behind the opposite leg. Turn in the opposite direction and move away with the ball using the opposite foot.

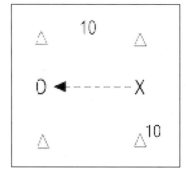

Practice Sequence 3

Individual running with ball handling

Layout:
For this practice set up grids of 10 X 30 yards.

In practice 3 set up a middle row of cones, each 2 to 3 yards apart depending on the ability of the players.

General:
The basic grids can be used for all three practices without any cones being moved.

Techniques for running with ball handling

Controlling the ball:
In practice 1 the control of the ball should be with the inside of the foot. The practice should be done with one touch with the ball being passed from one foot to the other.

In practice 2 the control of the ball should be with the bottom of the foot alternating the left and right foot.

In practice 3 the control of the ball should be with the inside of the foot. The practice should be done with the foot furthest away from the cones being used to pass the ball

General:
The players should be relaxed, keeping the head steady with eyes on the ball.
The body should be balanced, keeping the ball close to the feet and not letting the ball get away while running at a controlled speed.

KEY

Ball Movement	⟶	Player Movement	----➤
Attacking Player	X	Defending Player	O
Server	S	Goalkeeper	GK

Key Factors:
1. Close control of the ball
2. Eyes on the ball while controlling or kicking the ball
3. Good body balance
4. Run at controlled speed

EQUIPMENT: Grids created from cones, 10 Balls   TIME: 30 min.

Practice Sequence 1:
10 minutes
Each player take turns in running while alternately kicking the ball first with the right then the left foot.

Practice Sequence 1

Practice Sequence 2:
10 minutes
Each player take turns in running backwards while alternately dragging the ball with the top of the foot, first with the right then the left foot.

Practice Sequence 2

Practice Sequence 3:
10 minutes
Each player take turns running between the cones, kicking the ball between the cones, using the inside of the foot furthest away from the cones.

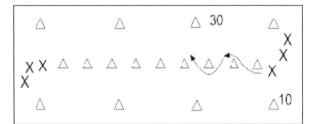

Practice Sequence 3

One touch practice

Layout:
The first practice can be made up of several grids of 10 X 10 yards to accommodate the whole team.
The second practice is 10 X 10 yard squares, so the first grid layout can be used.
For the third practice the same grid can be used and add the passing cones spaced at about 3 yards apart.

General:
In practice 1 and 2 make sure the players are actively moving, not just standing and passing.
The players should use just one touch of the ball, playing the ball directly to each other.

In practice 3 the passing should only be one touch but running speed and pace of the ball will effect the outcome of the pass.
The spacing of the cones will depend on the ability and age of the players.

Techniques for one touch ball control

Ground passing:
The foot is turned outward so that the inside of the boot makes contact with the ball at right angles to the line of the pass.

The ankle must be firm to create a hockey stick effect.

To keep the ball low, the contact of the boot on the ball should be through the horizontal mid-line of the ball, with the body over the ball.

The non-kicking foot should be placed alongside the ball far enough away to allow a free-swinging movement of the kicking leg.

The position of the head should be steady with eyes looking down at the ball.

KEY

Ball Movement	⟶	Player Movement	------➤
Attacking Player	X	Defending Player	0
Server	S	Goalkeeper	GK

Key Factors:

1. Eyes on the ball while kicking.
2. Body over the ball.
3. Non kicking foot square on the ball.
4. Pace and accuracy.

EQUIPMENT: GRIDS CREATED FROM CONES, 10 BALLS   **TIME:** 30 MIN.

Practice Sequence 1:

10 minutes
X passes to O using just one touch of the ball.
The ball is then passed between the players using just one touch with pace and accuracy.

Practice Sequence 2:

10 minutes
X1 passes to X2 who passes to X3.
X3 passes the ball back to X1 who passes to X4.
X4 passes to X3 who passes to X1.
Continue in this sequence.

Practice Sequence 3:

10 minutes
X and O run along the side of the cones passing the ball to each other between the cones but only using one touch of the ball.

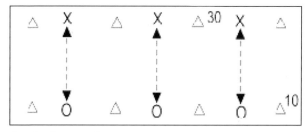

Practice Sequence 1

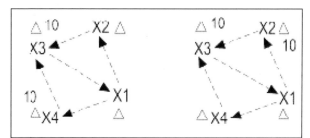

Practice Sequence 2

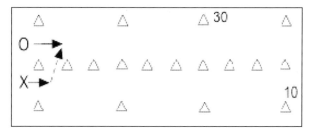

Practice Sequence 3

Passing and running

Layout:
For the first practice, set up enough grids of 15 X 15 yards with at least 4 players to a grid.
For the second practice set up grids of 20 X 20 yards with cones positioned half way along each side and use at least 8 players to a grid.

General:
In both practices the players should use 2 touches, the first touch to control the ball and the second to pass to the next player.

In practice 2 start off with one ball and when this is running well, introduce the second ball.

Techniques for passing, trapping and running

Ground Passes:
The foot is turned outward so that the inside of the boot makes contact with the ball at right angles to the line of the pass. The ankle must be firm to create a hockey stick effect.

Trapping with the foot:
Keep the foot at right angles to the ball with the body well over the ball, allowing the foot to swing back as the foot contacts the ball to cushion the impact.

Running without the ball:
Move quickly but at controlled speed to the next point to be ready to receive the ball.

KEY

Ball Movement	⟶	Player Movement	------>
Attacking Player	X	Defending Player	0
Server	S	Goalkeeper	GK

Key Factors:

1. A ground pass with accuracy and good pace
2. Trap the ball with one touch and pass the ball with the second touch
3. Keep body over the ball with eyes on the ball
4. Run at controlled speed in opposite direction to the ball

EQUIPMENT: GRIDS CREATED FROM CONES, 10 BALLS   **TIME: 30 MIN.**

Practice Sequence 1:

15 minutes
X1 passes to X2 and runs to join X4.
X2 receives the ball, passes to X3 and runs back to the cone vacated by X1.
X3 receives the ball, passes to X4 and runs back to the cone vacated by X2.
Continue the exercise using all players around the grid.

Practice Sequence 2:

15 minutes
Start the sequence with X1 and X5 and play with 2 balls.
X1 passes to X2 and runs to join X8.
At the same time X5 passes to X6 and runs to join X4.
X2 receives the ball, passes to X3 and runs back to the cone vacated by X1.
At the same time X6 receives the ball, passes to X7 and runs back to the cone vacated by X5.
Keep the play continuous but if the play gets out of sequence or the balls go out of the grid start again.

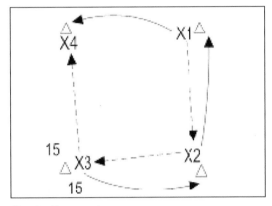

Practice Sequence 1

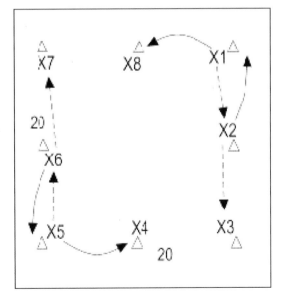

Practice Sequence 2

Ground passing accuracy

Layout:
For this practice, use half of a soccer field with the goal and penalty area.
Create a grid for practice 1 with cones the width of the penalty D and
10 yards beyond the penalty area.
In practice 2 extend the cones up to 20 yards beyond the penalty area.

General:
In practice 1 the players should only pass twice before shooting.
Start from both sides to practice the right and left passes.

In practice 2 the attacking player should run to the ball and away from the
goal, to set up the pass for the player to shoot on goal.

Techniques for ground passing

Passing:
The speed of the ball must have enough pace to reach its target but not so
much that it is difficult to control.
The timing of the pass should be to maximize the position of the player
receiving the pass and place the opponents at a disadvantage.

Running:
The player should make a controlled run, always expecting the ball to be
passed.
The run should be into space created by the player who was passed the ball.

KEY

Ball Movement	⟶	Player Movement	⟶
Attacking Player	X	Defending Player	0
Server	S	Goalkeeper	GK

Key Factors:
1. Ground passes with accuracy and pace
2. When passing keep the eyes on the ball with the body up and over the ball
3. Run at controlled speed to the next point to receive the ball.
4. Be relaxed and confident to pass and receive the ball.

EQUIPMENT: GOAL AND PENALTY AREA, 10 BALLS, BIBS

TIME: 30 MIN.

Practice Sequence 1:
15 minutes
The server plays the ball to X1 who controls the ball and runs to make a pass through the cones to X2.
X2 runs alongside the cones to receive the ball half way along the grid area.
X1 continues running to receive the return pass from X2 and takes a shot on goal.
Alternate the start right and left.

Practice Sequence 2:
15 minutes
The server plays the ball to X1 who controls the ball and runs to make a pass through the cones to X2.
X2 starts at the opposite side of the grid and runs towards X1 to receive the ball.
X1 continues running to receive the return pass from X2 and a makes a shot on goal.
Alternate the start right and left.

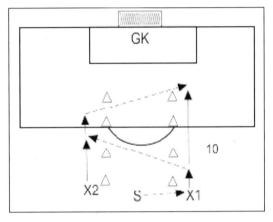

Practice Sequence 1

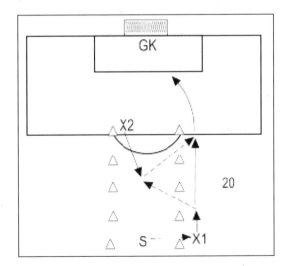

Practice Sequence 2

Lofted forward passing

Layout:

In practice 1 the grids should be 4 to 5 yards square and enough to accommodate the whole team but keep the number of players in each grid to 2 or 3.

In practice 2 place the 5 X 5 yard target areas on the corners of the penalty area and make the outside grid 20 yards beyond the penalty area.

General:

In practice 1 work on accuracy of the pass with both the right and left foot.

In practice 2 the X player should get in front of the defender and be first to the ball.

Once the X player has the ball under control he should be prepared to shoot or dribble and score a goal.

Techniques for lofted passing

Kicking with the instep:
The ankle of the kicking foot should be extended and firm and contact the ball through the vertical mid-line and through the bottom half of the ball.
Kicking with the inside of the foot:
The foot should be pointed outward with the ankle firm and extended and the foot should strike the ball through the bottom half.
Kicking with the outside of the foot:
The foot should come across the body from outside to inside making contact with the bottom half of the ball.

General:
The non-kicking foot should be slightly behind and positioned about one foot to the side of the ball.

The position of the head should be steady with eyes looking down at the ball while kicking.

KEY

Ball Movement	⟶		Player Movement	------➤
Attacking Player	X		Defending Player	0
Server	S		Goalkeeper	GK

Key Factors:

1. Head up to view the field of play
2. Play a forward lofted pass
3. Timing and accuracy of the pass
4. Play to the receiving player or in front, for the player to run on to.

EQUIPMENT: GOAL AND PENALTY AREA, 10 BALLS, BIBS

TIME: 30 MIN.

Practice Sequence 1:

10 minutes
The players take turns making a lofted pass into the opposing square.
The players make lofted passes to each other concentrating on the lofted passing technique. Encourage players to alternate using both the left and right foot.

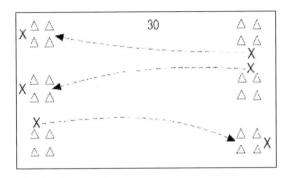

Practice Sequence 1

Practice Sequence 2:

20 minutes
X1 passes the ball to server and runs to receive the returned pass. X2 runs across the field to receive a lofted pass in the far corner of the penalty area.
The O players should defend to prevent a shot on goal.
Alternate the start both left and right.

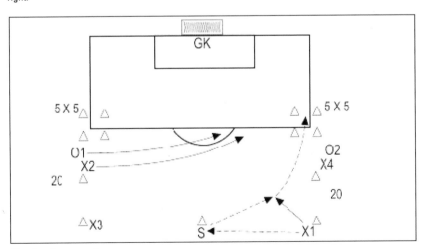

Practice Sequence 2

Running with the ball

Layout:
For practice 1 make grids 10 X 20 yards with 3 gates made of cones about 3 yards apart for the players to run through.

In practice 2 make grids of 20 X 20 yards using 6 cones 10 yards apart from each other.
The distance for each player to run between the cones should be 20 yards.

For practice 3 make an overall grid of 20 X 40 yards including 2 end grids of 20 X 10 and a running zone of 20 X 20. The 2 end grids are for the X players to play against the O players and attempt to release one of their team to run with the ball through the running zone and join the other X players in the other end grid.

General:
If any of the practices get confusing, start the practice again.

Techniques for running with the ball

Running with the Ball:
Run quickly at controlled speed kicking the ball with the outside of the foot.

Between kicking the ball look up to view the situation.

Before coming into tackling distance of an opponent make a decision to either pass or cross the ball if shooting for a goal is not viable.

Be prepared to run with the ball but not necessarily dribble. Keep out of tackling distance.

KEY

Ball Movement	⟶		Player Movement	⇢
Attacking Player	X		Defending Player	0
Server	S		Goalkeeper	GK

Key Factors:

1. Kick the ball into space in front with the outside of the foot.
2. Run quickly but at controlled speed.
3. Avoid opponents by running into space.
4. Keep head up while not kicking the ball to view the field.

EQUIPMENT: GRIDS CREATED FROM CONES, 10 BALLS, BIBS

TIME: 30 MIN.

Practice Sequence 1:

10 minutes
One player at a time collects the ball and runs through the gates at controlled speed.
The ball is played to the next player and the first player joins the team.

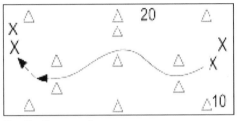

Practice Sequence 1

Practice Sequence 2:

10 minutes
One player from each of the three teams takes turns in crossing the grid running with the ball, avoiding other players without losing the ball.
When the player reaches the other side of the grid the ball is passed to the next player.

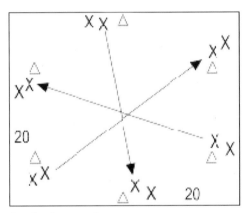

Practice Sequence 2

Practice Sequence 3:

10 minutes
The object of the practice is for the X players in one end grid to play against the O players and release one of their team to run with the ball through the running zone and join the other X players in the other end grid. To start, the O player in the running zone passes the ball to an X player in the end grid with the most X players, and the X team should play against the O players to release one of them from the grid to run with the ball through the running zone. The O defenders must stay inside their respective grids but prevent the X players from releasing one of their players into running zone. The O player in the running zone is not allowed outside this area and must prevent the X player from running through the running zone and join the X players in the other end grid. If the ball goes out of the grid start again.

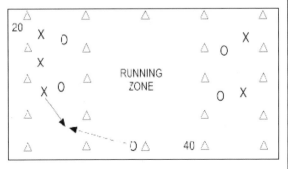

Practice Sequence 3

Defending by marking players

Layout:
Set up the first practice with grids 40 X 10.
The second and third practices should be square grids of 15 X 15 yards.
The second practice should have 2 goals of 2 to 3 yards in width.

General:
In the first practice make sure the player slows down before reaching the cone and then skips sideways.

The second and third practice should have four players at one time in the grid and change over after 2 to 3 minutes.

Techniques for defending and support

Defending:
The defending player should watch the ball when in a challenging position.

It is important for the defending player to adopt the ideal position two to three feet from the attacker.

The defender should be patient and concentrate on selecting the correct moment to tackle, the best moment being when the attacker attempts to turn.

Supporting player:
The supporting player should be positioned at an angle behind the defender, where the attacker is being sent.

The supporting player should communicate with the defender.

KEY

Ball Movement	⟶	Player Movement	- - - ->
Attacking Player	X	Defending Player	0
Server	S	Goalkeeper	GK

Key Factors:
1. Travel quickly when the ball is played to the opponent to be defended.
2. Slow down when closing in on the opponent.
3. Prevent the ball being played forward.
4. Recover defensive position when the ball is played.

EQUIPMENT: GRIDS CREATED FROM CONES, 10 BALLS, BIBS

TIME: 30 MIN.

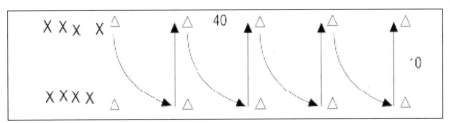

Practice Sequence 1

Practice Sequence 1:
10 minutes
Run in a half circle to the opposite cone, slowing down before the cone. Side skip to the cone opposite, facing the same direction. The first player goes right, the second player left, and alternate the players around.

Practice Sequence 2:
10 minutes
The X players can pass to each other but the O players must prevent either of the X players from shooting at one of the goals at the furthest end of the grid.

Practice Sequence 3:
10 minutes
The X players can pass to each other but the O players must prevent either of the X players from passing forward to the forward X player. The forward X player can move from side to side to receive the ball.

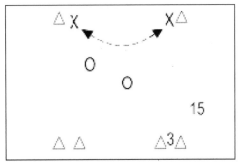

Practice Sequence 2

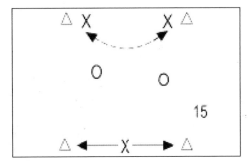

Practice Sequence 3

Prevent an opponent from turning

Layout:
In practice 1 use a goal and penalty area and create a grid of 20 X 30 yards from the end line.

In practice 2 extend the grid area to 30 X 30 yards to accommodate the two extra players.

General:
Make sure the defender O marks the attacker X closely. The practice should be as realistic as possible in the confines of the grid area

Switch players around to give all players the opportunity to practice.

Techniques for preventing an opponent from turning

Prevent an opponent from turning:

Always keep goal side of the opponent and occupy space.

When the opponent receives the ball, the defender should close the space quickly to prevent giving the player the opportunity to turn and face the goal.

Do not run into the opponent but rather stop within 1 to 1.5 yards of him, keeping both him and the ball in view.

The supporting defender should be close enough to challenge the opponent when the ball is passed, but in a position to support the defender on the ball.

The defender should force the opponent to defensive strength or out of the grid area.

KEY

Ball Movement	⟶		Player Movement	------➤
Attacking Player	X		Defending Player	0
Server	S		Goalkeeper	GK

Key Factors:

1. Close down the space quickly between defender and opponent.
2. Keep goal side of the ball and be patient.
3. Be close enough to prevent the opponent from turning.
4. Steer opponent to the supporting player.

EQUIPMENT: Goal and Penalty Area, 10 Balls, Bibs, Cones   TIME: 30 min.

Practice Sequence 1:

15 minutes

The servers take turns passing the ball to either X1 or X2.

The X player should run to receive the ball from the server.

The other X player should create space to receive the ball.

The players should only play in the grid area and if the ball goes out the server should play another ball.

Practice Sequence 2:

15 minutes

The servers take turns passing the ball to either X1, X2 or X3.

The X player should run to receive the ball from the server.

The other 2 X players should create space to receive the ball.

The players should only play in the grid area and if the ball goes out the server should play another ball.

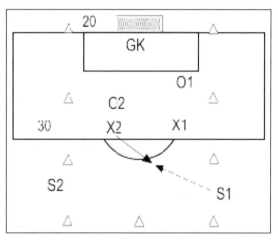

Practice Sequence 1

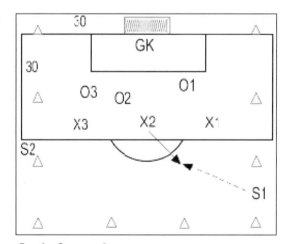

Practice Sequence 2

Ball handling in an attacking position

Layout:
Use grids of 20 X 30 yards with a goal made up of 2 cones 8 yards apart on one side of the grid.
Use enough grids to accommodate the whole team.

General:
The X players should attempt a first time shot or header on goal from the throw-in.

In the fourth practice add a defender and allow the attackers to select the type of attack on goal.

Techniques and skills for ball handling in an attacking position

Attacking around the goal:

The first choice of an attacking player in the penalty area is to accept the responsibility to shoot.

Players should not be afraid of a physical challenge and should be prepared to perform difficult techniques around the goal.

Missing the target should not put players off from shooting again.

Different techniques should be encouraged:
- Receiving the ball and turning in one movement
- Moving in one direction and checking and moving away from the opponent
- Shooting around opponents
- Feinting before shooting to unbalance the opponent.

KEY				
Ball Movement	⟶		Player Movement	⇢
Attacking Player	X		Defending Player	0
Server	S		Goalkeeper	GK

Key Factors:

1. Keep your eye on the ball.
2. Keep the body square to the incoming ball.
3. Have courage to attack the ball.
4. Decision on technique to use.

EQUIPMENT: GRIDS CREATED FROM CONES, 10 BALLS

TIME: 40 MIN.

Practice Sequence 1:

10 minutes

The server throws the ball at head height to the X player who heads the ball to score a goal.

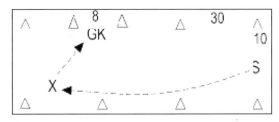

Practice Sequence 1

Practice Sequence 2:

10 minutes

The server throws the ball to the X player who traps the ball with the chest and shoots first time with the foot.

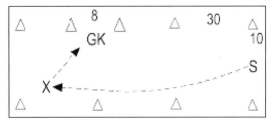

Practice Sequence 2

Practice Sequence 3:

10 minutes

The server throws the ball at waist height to the X player who makes a diving header for a shot on goal

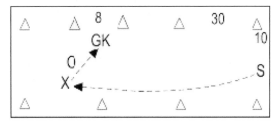

Practice Sequence 3

Practice Sequence 4:

10 minutes

The server throws the ball to the X player who makes a decision which technique to use.

The O player defends the goal.

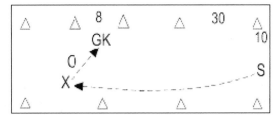

Practice Sequence 4

Running and shooting

Layout:
Set up grids 30 X 40 yards with 2 goals made of cones or use actual goals where possible at each end.
In practice 1, set up gates on each side of the grid at 5 yards apart.
These gates can vary in position to make it easier or harder to shoot on the goal.
In practice 2, lay out 3 cones on each side of the grid for the players to dribble through.
The distance between the cones will depend on the age and skill level of the players.

General:
There should be enough time for the goalkeeper to collect the ball and throw it to the next player before the next player takes a shot.
Each player should retrieve his own ball to allow the goalkeepers to concentrate on the practice.

The sequence should flow, even if extra balls are needed by the goalkeeper.

Techniques for shooting

Shooting with the instep:
The ankle of the kicking foot should be extended and firm and contact the ball through the vertical mid-line of the ball, with the body over the ball.

Shooting with inside of the foot:
The foot should be pointed outward with the ankle firm and extended, with the body over the ball.

General:
The non-kicking foot should be placed alongside the ball but far enough away to allow a free-swinging movement of the kicking leg.
The position of the head should be steady with eyes looking down at the ball.

KEY			
Ball Movement	⟶	Player Movement	- - - - - -⟶
Attacking Player	X	Defending Player	0
Server	S	Goalkeeper	GK

Key Factors:

1. Run at a controlled speed
2. Check the position of the goalkeeper
3. Eyes on the ball with body over the ball and do not overreach
4. Shoot for accuracy rather than power.

EQUIPMENT: GOAL AND PENALTY AREA, 10 BALLS, BIBS, CONES   **TIME**: 30 MIN.

Practice Sequence 1:

15 minutes

The goalkeeper throws the ball to the next X player who controls the ball with the first touch and shoots with the next touch.

The X player should wait until the goalkeeper is ready.

The X players should retrieve their own ball after each shot.

Practice Sequence 2:

15 minutes

The goalkeeper throws the ball to the next X player who controls the ball, dribbles around the cones and shoots on exiting the three cones.

The X player should wait until the goalkeeper is ready.

The X players should retrieve their own ball after each shot.

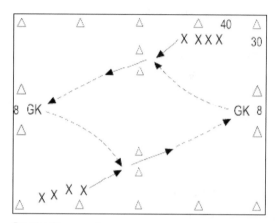

Practice Sequence 1

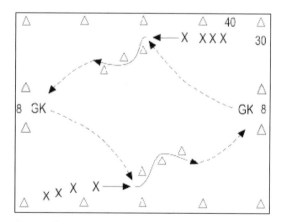

Practice Sequence 2

Turning and creating space to shoot

Layout:
This practice should be set up using an actual goal and penalty area.

The grid for practice 1 and 2 should be 20 X 20 yards, for practice 3 the grid should be extended to 20 X 30 yards to accommodate the extra players.

General:
Make sure the defenders O mark the attackers X closely and play as realistically as possible in the confines of the grid area

Switch players around to give all players the opportunity to practice.

Skills and techniques for turning and creating space to shoot

Creating space to shoot:
The player should draw the opponent to create space behind the opponent.

The player should move at a controlled speed towards the oncoming ball and suddenly increase pace before getting to the ball.

The player can receive the ball face on but has to turn 180 degrees to see the goal, or receive the ball at an angle which allows the player more vision of the space around the goal.

The player should receive the ball with the foot furthest away from the opponent and be ready to turn immediately.

KEY

Ball Movement	⟶		Player Movement	------→
Attacking Player	X		Defending Player	0
Server	S		Goalkeeper	GK

Key Factors:

1. Create space from the opponent by running sideways onto the ball
2. Receive the ball with the foot furthest away from opponent.
3. Turn and receive the ball in one move and shoot at first opportunity.
4. Supporting player runs to create space to receive the ball.

EQUIPMENT: GOAL AND PENALTY AREA, 10 BALLS, BIBS, CONES   **TIME: 30 MIN.**

Practice Sequence 1:

10 minutes

The X player runs to receive the ball from one of the servers, controls the ball and shoots.

Practice with players coming from both sides of the goal.

Practice Sequence 2:

10 minutes

The X player runs to receive the ball from one of the servers, controls the ball and shoots.

The O player acts a defender to prevent the X player from turning.

Practice with players coming from both sides of the goal.

Practice Sequence 3:

10 minutes

One of the X players runs to collect the ball from one of the servers, while the other X player creates space to receive a possible pass.

Both X players play together for a shot on goal.

The O players defend to prevent the X players from scoring.

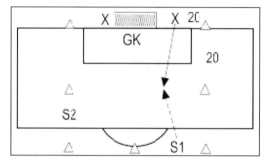

Practice Sequence 1

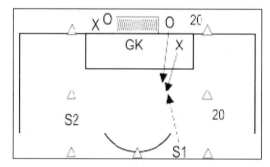

Practice Sequence 2

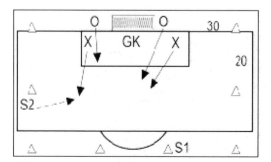

Practice Sequence 3

65

Attacking in front of the goal

Layout:
For practice 1 and 2 use a 10 X 30 yards grid with a goal of 8 yards at one side of the grid.
For practice 3 use an actual goal and penalty area where possible to make the practice realistic.

General:
The X players should attempt a first time shot or header on goal from the pass, but even if it is a bad pass the players should make an attempt on the goal.
In practice 2 add an extra attacker and a defender.
In practice 3 give the advantage to the attacking players with at least a 3 v 2 situation.
The center server should have enough balls to play as soon as the ball goes out of the grid.

Skills and techniques for attacking in front of the goal

Attacking the ball:
The first choice of an attacking player in the penalty area is to accept the responsibility to shoot.

Players should not be afraid of a physical challenge and should be prepared to perform difficult techniques around the goal.

Missing the target should not prevent players from shooting again.

Different techniques should be encouraged:
- Receiving the ball and turning in one movement
- Moving in one direction and checking and moving away from the opponent
- Shooting around opponents
- Feinting before shooting to unbalance the opponent.

KEY

Ball Movement	⟶		Player Movement	----➤
Attacking Player	X		Defending Player	0
Server	S		Goalkeeper	GK

Key Factors:

1. Create space to receive the ball
2. Attack the ball with the head or foot.
3. The timing of the run or movement to the ball.
4. Get in front of the defender and be first to the ball.

EQUIPMENT: GOAL AND PENALTY AREA, GRIDS CREATED FROM CONES, 10 BALLS

TIME: 30 MIN.

Practice Sequence 1:

10 minutes
The server makes a lofted pass to the X player who attacks the ball to score a goal.
The O players defend to prevent the X players from scoring.

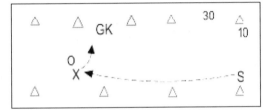

Practice Sequence 1

Practice Sequence 2:

10 minutes
The server makes a lofted pass to the X players who attack the ball to score a goal.
The O players defend to prevent the X players from scoring.

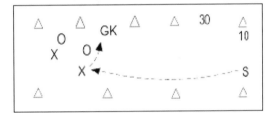

Practice Sequence 2

Practice Sequence 3:

10 minutes
The center server passes to one of the servers at the side of the penalty area, who then makes a ground or lofted pass into the penalty area.
The X players inside the penalty area should attempt to score while the O players defend.

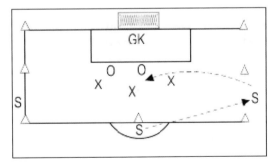

Practice Sequence 3

Goalkeeping shots

Layout:
This practice should be set up using an actual goal and penalty area.

The grid should be set up inside the penalty area and be about 45 degrees to the goal and then directly to the top of the circle.

General:
In practice 2 the shooting players should move the ball around to make the goalkeeper move across the goal but should shoot from the edge of the grid.

In practice 3 keep the play as realistic as possible although it is a 4 v 2 situation, giving the advantage to the attacking players to produce more shots on goal.

Make sure enough balls are available so that the goalkeeper does not have to fetch the ball.

Skills and techniques for goalkeeping shots

Moving into line:
The goalkeeper should use a sideways skipping motion with one foot coming to the other foot before the other foot is moved again.

The goalkeeper should always be in line with the ball and the cone placed at the middle and rear of the goal.

General:
The hands should be behind the ball with palms facing outward

With the exception of the kneeling technique, the feet should be shoulder width apart, with the head steady and eyes on the ball as long as possible.

KEY			
Ball Movement	⟶	Player Movement	- - - - -▶
Attacking Player	X	Defending Player	0
Server	S	Goalkeeper	GK

Key Factors:

1. Goalkeeper position
2. Skip across the goal with body square to the ball.
3. Eyes on the ball and body balanced with the palms facing outwards.
4. Communicate with defenders.

EQUIPMENT: GOAL AND PENALTY AREA, 10 BALLS, BIBS, CONES

TIME: 30 MIN.

Practice Sequence 1:

10 minutes
The server shoots at the goalkeeper from different positions.
Check goalkeeper techniques and skills when necessary.

Practice Sequence 2:

10 minutes
The X players pass to each other to make the goalkeeper move across the goal.
The X players may shoot at will.

Practice Sequence 3:

10 minutes
The goalkeeper throws the ball to the X players who play to each other for a good shot on goal. The O players defend the goal while communicating with the goalkeeper.

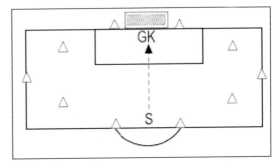

Practice Sequence 1

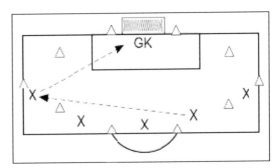

Practice Sequence 2

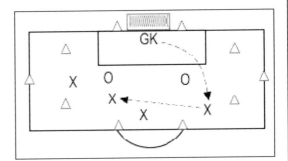

Practice Sequence 3

Passing as a group

Layout:
In practice 1 the two cones are 10 yards apart.
In practice 2 the grids are 10 X 10 yards.
In practice 3 the grid is 20 X 20 yards with 4 goals, one in each corner at 3 yards apart.

General:
In practice 1 keep the number of players to 4 or 5 and limit to 2 touches of the ball, if possible.

In practice 2 the X players are only allowed to run between 2 cones and are restricted to 2 touches of the ball and a maximum of 10 passes. The O player should threaten the X players while the ball is being passed.

In practice 3 the X players defend 2 of the goals and the O players the other 2. This practice is 4 v 4 which can also include touch restriction. There are no goalkeepers needed in the practice as all are field players.

Skills for passing as a group

Passing:
Passes should be made at the correct pace and angle to allow space to be created and exploited.

Supporting players:
The supporting players should adopt a good position to receive the ball from a player under pressure, so that a forward pass can be made between the opponents.

The distance between the player with the ball and the supporting player, should be great enough to give the supporting player time to make a forward run, but not so great that the opponent has time to recover.

KEY				
Ball Movement	⟶		Player Movement	------▶
Attacking Player	X		Defending Player	0
Server	S		Goalkeeper	GK

Key Factors:
1. Passes should be accurate and with good pace.
2. First touch on the ball.
3. Control the ball in the direction of the run.
4. Create space off the ball to receive a pass.

EQUIPMENT: Grids created from cones, 10 Balls, Bibs   **TIME:** 30 min.

Practice Sequence 1:

10 minutes
The X players should pass the ball to the opposite X player and then run to the end of the other line.
Count the number of passes before the ball is lost, for competition.

Practice Sequence 2:

10 minutes
The X players should try to make 10 consecutive passes to each other across the grid then rotate the defender.
If the defender intercepts the ball then the defender is rotated automatically. The X players are only allowed to run between the cones.

Practice Sequence 3:

10 minutes
4 v 4 inside a 20 X 20 yard grid with four goals.
The X players should attack the 2 goals to the right and the O players should attack the 2 goals to left.

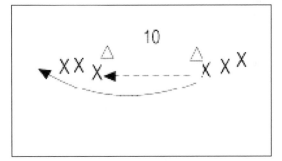

Practice Sequence 1

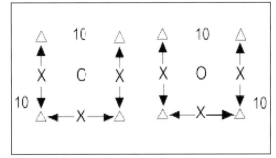

Practice Sequence 2

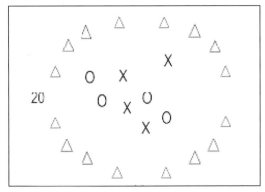

Practice Sequence 3

Creating space with overlap running

Layout:
Use an actual goal and penalty area plus a grid outside the area, which should be the width of the penalty area and 40 yards from the end line.

General:
The sequence can take place starting to the left and then the right and then alternate.

The defenders in practice 2 should not start before the attacker but must threaten the play.

X2 should start on the first cone 10 yards from X1 and X3 should start on the second cone 20 yards from X1.

Skills for creating space with overlap running

Passing:
The pace on the ball should be sufficient to reach its target but not so much that it is difficult to control.

The timing of the pass should be to maximize the position of the player receiving the pass, and place the opponents at a disadvantage.

Running:
The player should make a controlled run outside of the player who was passed the ball, and always expect a return pass.

The run should be into space created by the player who was passed the ball, and behind the opponent.

KEY

Ball Movement	⟶	Player Movement	----➤
Attacking Player	X	Defending Player	0
Server	S	Goalkeeper	GK

Key Factors:

1. Run outside the player who was passed the ball.
2. Player communications.
3. Timing of the pass.
4. Run behind the opponent to create space.

EQUIPMENT: GOAL AND PENALTY AREA, 10 BALLS, BIBS, CONES

TIME: 30 MIN.

Practice Sequence 1:

15 minutes

X1 runs to collect the pass from the server.

X2 runs to collect the pass from X1.

X3 runs to collect the pass from X2 while X1 makes an overlap run outside of X2.

X2 then makes an overlap around X3. X1 collects the pass from X3 and attacks the goal.

Practice Sequence 2:

15 minutes

X1 runs to collect the pass from the server.

X2 runs to collect the pass from X1.

X3 runs to collect the pass from X2 while X1 makes an overlap run outside of X2.

X2 then makes an overlap around X3. X1 collects the pass from X3 and attacks the goal.

The 2 defenders should prevent the X players from making the passes.

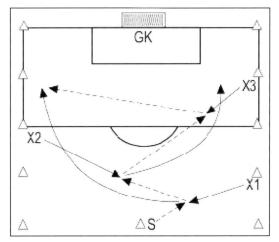

Practice Sequence 1

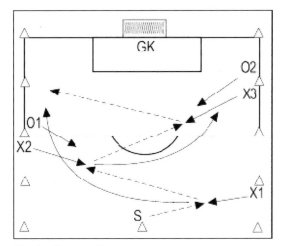

Practice Sequence 2

Creating space with wall passes

Layout:
Use an actual goal and penalty area plus a grid outside the area, which should be the width of the penalty area and 40 yards from the end line.

General:
The sequence can take place starting first to the left and then the right, then alternate.

The defenders in practice 2 should not start before the attacker X1 has collected the ball, but should threaten the play.

X2 should start on the first cone (10 yards from X1) and X3 should start on the second cone (20 yards from X1).

Skills for wall passing

Passing:
The player with the ball should run at the opponent and release the pass just before being tackled by the opponent.

The pace on the ball should be enough to reach its target but not so much that it is difficult to control.

The timing of the pass should be to maximize the position of the player receiving the pass and place the opponents at a disadvantage.

Running:
The player should make a controlled run, always expecting the ball to be passed into space behind the opponents.

Positioning:
The wall pass supporting player should be positioned at a good angle and distance from the opponents to receive the ball.

KEY

Ball Movement		Player Movement	
Attacking Player	X	Defending Player	0
Server	S	Goalkeeper	GK

Key Factors:

1. Player with the ball should run directly at the opponent.
2. The timing of the pass should draw the opponent to create space.
3. After passing, make a run into space behind the opponent.
4. The return pass should be in front of the attacking player.

EQUIPMENT: GOAL AND PENALTY AREA, 10 BALLS, BIBS, CONES　　　**TIME:** 30 MIN.

Practice Sequence 1:

15 minutes
The server passes to X1.
X2 runs to collect the pass from X1.
X2 passes back to X1 who has made
a run to into space.
X3 runs to collect the pass from X1.
X3 passes back to X1 who has made
a run into the penalty area to shoot
the ball.

Practice Sequence 2:

15 minutes
The server passes to X1.
X2 runs to collect the pass from X1.
X1 makes a run into space behind the
defender O1 to collect the ball and
shoot.
X3 runs to create space for X1.
Both O1 and O2 should defend to pre-
vent a goal.

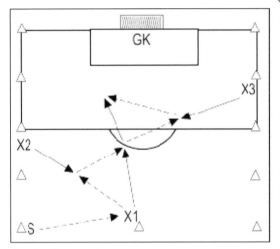

Practice Sequence 1

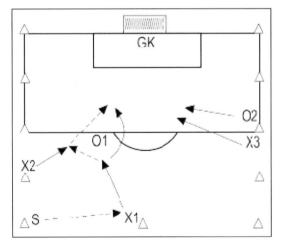

Practice Sequence 2

Active shooting

Layout:
This practice should be set up as a 40 X 40 yards grid with goals and goal-keepers. This will give the impression of 2 penalty areas back to back.

General:
Start the practice with the 4 players in the back part of the grid moving the ball toward the middle line and shooting at the first opportunity. In the 4 v 2 situation, this should happen very quickly.

In practice 2 allow the 2 forward players the opportunity to either pass back or shoot first time.

Skills for active shooting

Attitude:
The players must take responsibility and shoot whenever possible.

Missing the target should not deter the player from shooting again, as missing an opportunity to shoot is worse than missing the target.

Shoot with determination to score a goal.

Shooting:
Accuracy is more important than power even over a great distance.

The shot should be within the range of the players' ability.

Check the position of the goalkeeper and the opponents before shooting.

Do not shoot if an opponent can block the shot, pass to a player who has a better opportunity to shoot.

KEY

Ball Movement	⟶		Player Movement	⇢
Attacking Player	X		Defending Player	0
Server	S		Goalkeeper	GK

Key Factors:

1. Check the position of the goalkeeper.
2. Accuracy over power.
3. Shoot on first opportunity if within range and not blocked by an opponent.
4. If it is not possible to shoot, pass to a player with a better opportunity.

EQUIPMENT: 2 GOALS AND GRID 40 x 40, 10 BALLS, BIBS, CONES   TIME: 30 MIN.

Practice Sequence 1:

15 minutes

The goalkeeper throws the ball to a teammate.

Any player can shoot from the back grid.

The 2 O or X players in the forward grid can only pass back to their players in the back grid.

All players must stay inside their half of the practice grid.

Practice Sequence 2:

15 minutes

Any X player or O player can shoot from the back grid.

The 2 O or X players in the forward grid can continue to pass back to their players in the back grid or a one touch shot on goal.

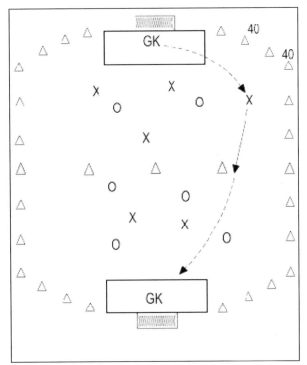

Practice Sequence 1

When and when not to shoot

Layout:
Use a goal and penalty area with a V shaped coned area. The angle of the V shaped grid should be positioned so that shooting outside of the cones is not a good shooting angle for the players involved. This can depend on the age and the ability of the players.

General:
The defending players should threaten realistically to prevent the shot.

Encourage the players to shoot at the first good opportunity.

Change the practice by starting from the left and then the right side.

Skills for when and when not to shoot

When to shoot:
Shoot inside the coned area in front of the goal, within the range of the player's ability, if a defender is not blocking the shooting possibility.

When not to shoot:
When an opponent is so close as to be certain to block the shot.

When the distance is so great that it gives an unacceptable percentage chance of missing the target.

When the angle is so small that it gives an unacceptable chance of scoring a goal.

KEY

Ball Movement	⟶		Player Movement	----➤
Attacking Player	X		Defending Player	0
Server	S		Goalkeeper	GK

Key Factors:
1. Shoot inside the shooting area.
2. Shoot within the range of the players' ability.
3. Do not shoot if an opponent can block the shot.
4. Dribble or pass the ball from outside the shooting area.

EQUIPMENT: GOAL AND PENALTY AREA, 10 BALLS, BIBS, CONES

TIME: 30 MIN.

Practice Sequence 1:
15 minutes

X1 passes to the server who passes the ball to X2 .

X2 should shoot if possible inside the shooting area, otherwise dribble or pass into the area for a shot. The defender O can threaten X2 as soon as the server passes the ball.

Practice Sequence 2:
15 minutes

X1 passes to the server.

The server passes to either X2 or X3 who should shoot if possible, otherwise pass to one of the other attackers.

The two defenders O1 and O2 can threaten the attacking players as soon as the ball is passed from X1.

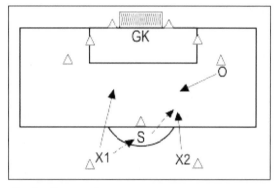

Practice Sequence 1

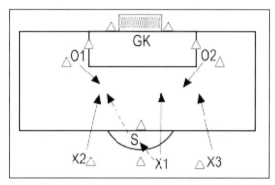

Practice Sequence 2

Attacking one on one with the goalkeeper

Layout:
Use a goal and penalty area.

In practice 1, set up one cone where players begin and one where the server should stand.

In practice 2, set up three cones for the attacking players, one on each edge of the penalty area and one 10 yards away from the middle of the penalty area.

General:
In practice 2 the defenders should threaten the attacking players without creating a foul.

Keep a player time limit in both practices. Practice 1 should be a maximum of 10 seconds and practice 2 a maximum of 25 to 30 seconds.

Skills for attacking one on one with the goalkeeper

Checking the goalkeeper:
The attacker should check the position of the goalkeeper and observe the speed and angle of the goalkeeper's movements to determine the space available to shoot.

Attacking player:
The attacker should bring the ball under control quickly and play the ball in front.

Make a decision either to shoot the ball after assessing the position of the goalkeeper, or to dribble around the goalkeeper and shoot after the goalkeeper is beaten.

KEY

Ball Movement	⟶	Player Movement	------➤
Attacking Player	X	Defending Player	O
Server	S	Goalkeeper	GK

Key Factors:
1. Bring ball under control in front of the body and play it forward.
2. Check the position and movement of the goalkeeper.
3. Run at controlled speed.
4. Make decision to shoot or dribble.

EQUIPMENT: Goal and penalty area, 10 Balls, Bibs, Cones   TIME: 30 min.

Practice Sequence 1:

15 minutes

Each X player takes a turn passing the ball to the server and runs into position to collect the ball.

The goalkeeper should close the angle of the attacker. Keep a time limit of 10 seconds.

Practice Sequence 2:

15 minutes

The server passes the ball to X1.

The X players play the ball to free up one of the players to make a move toward the goal.

The defending O players are active as soon as the ball is played by the server to threaten the attackers. Keep a time limit of 25 to 30 seconds.

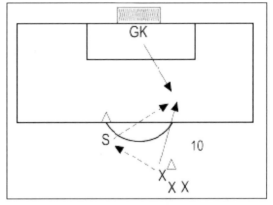

Practice Sequence 1

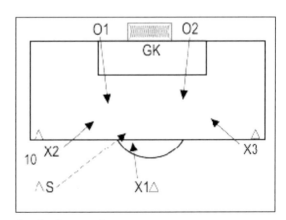

Practice Sequence 2

Defending the penalty area

Layout:
For this practice use the goal and penalty area. The cones for the crossing players should be 40 yards from the end line and 10 yards from the side line on both sides.

General:
In practice 1 the crossing players X1 and X2 should take turns crossing the ball into the penalty area. All players should come into the penalty area in pairs from behind the goal and return to the sideline after moving out of the penalty area.

In practice 2 the attacking players should threaten the defenders and try to score a goal when possible.

Skills for defending the penalty area

Defending around the penalty area:
The defending players should move to the ball first and attack it at its highest point.

The defenders should play the ball clear of any attacking players.

The ball should be played high, long and wide and into the opposite direction from which it came.

The defenders should move out of the goal area after clearing the ball, placing the opposing players in an offside position.

KEY

Ball Movement	⟶		Player Movement	------>
Attacking Player	X		Defending Player	0
Server	S		Goalkeeper	GK

Key Factors:
1. Move to the ball first and attack it at its highest trajectory.
2. Play the ball clear of the attacking player.
3. Play the ball in the opposite direction from which it came.
4. Move out of the penalty area after clearing.

EQUIPMENT: GOAL AND PENALTY AREA, 10 BALLS, BIBS, CONES

TIME: 30 MIN.

Practice Sequence 1:

15 minutes
The server plays the ball to X1 or X2 who makes a cross into the penalty area.
The O players should play the ball out of the penalty area.

Practice Sequence 2:

15 minutes
The server passes the ball to X1 or X2 who take turns crossing the ball into the penalty area.
O1, O2 and O3 should defend the penalty area with the goalkeeper, while X3 and X4 attempt to score a goal.

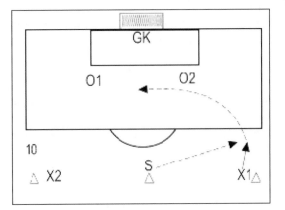

Practice Sequence 1

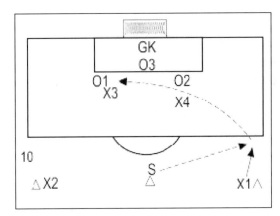

Practice Sequence 2

Defending as a team

Layout:
Use an actual goal and penalty area plus a grid outside the area, which should be the width of the penalty area and 40 yards from the end line.

General:
In practice 1 the defenders O1 and O2 should act as a 2 player defense and prevent the attacking players X1 and X2 from scoring a goal.

In practice 2 the ball can be played to any of the attackers by the server. Different players should be served from varying positions and with a different pace on the ball, to change the situations.

As soon as the ball is played by the server, the practice sequence starts.

If the ball goes out of the grid area, the practice sequence is finished.

Skills for defending as a team

Team Defending:
The defenders should keep both the opposing players and the ball in view at all times.

The defenders should always turn into the play and never have their backs towards the ball or the opposing players.

Deny space to the back of the defense and keep the opposition playing square or in front of the defense.

The defenders should always be close enough to the opposing players to close down the space when the ball is passed.

KEY				
Ball Movement	⟶		Player Movement	- - - - -▸
Attacking Player	X		Defending Player	0
Server	S		Goalkeeper	GK

Key Factors:

1. The opposition should always be kept in front of the defense.
2. Keep both the opposing players and the ball in view.
3. Always turn into the play.
4. Deny space to the back of the defense.

EQUIPMENT: Goal and penalty area, 10 Balls, Bibs, Cones   TIME: 30 min.

Practice Sequence 1:

15 minutes

The server passes the ball to X1 who then plays with X2 while the defenders O1 and O2 defend as a team.

Practice Sequence 2:

15 minutes

The server passes the ball to X1 who then plays with the other attacking players X2, X3 and X4 while the defenders O1, O2, O3 and O4 defend as a team creating a 4 v 4 situation.

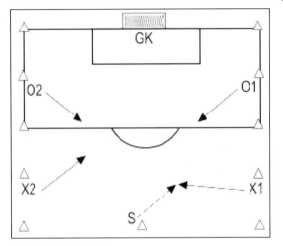

Practice Sequence 1

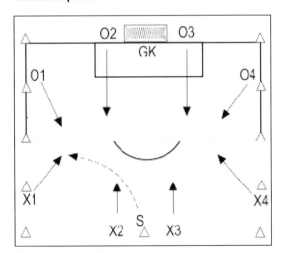

Practice Sequence 2

Diagonal passing and running in attack

Layout:
Use an actual goal and penalty area plus a grid outside the area, which should be the width of the penalty area, and 30 yards from the end line for practice 1, and 40 yards for practice 2.

The playing grid in practice 1 should be 10 X 20 yards situated in front of the penalty area, in line with the goal area.

General:
In practice 1 keep the play flowing and start the sequence alternatively right and left.

In practice 2 start the sequence alternatively right and left. When X1 has played the ball to X3, the player should take up the position vacated by X3 and be in the next sequence with two new players.

Skills for diagonal passing and running

Passing:
The passes should be played to an oncoming player or into space behind a defender, for the attacking player to run onto.

The receiving player should control the ball quickly to give himself time to decide what is the next move.

Timed accurate passes create space for the receiving players.

Running:
The players should create space by running towards the player with the ball or by running into space behind the defense.

The runs should always be diagonally across the field.

	KEY		
Ball Movement	⟶	Player Movement	------→
Attacking Player	X	Defending Player	0
Server	S	Goalkeeper	GK

Key Factors:
1. Timing and accuracy of the pass and pace on the ball.
2. Timing and angle of the runs.
3. Runs should be diagonal and across the field.
4. Create space by running to the ball or behind an opponent.

EQUIPMENT: GOAL AND PENALTY AREA, 10 BALLS, BIBS, CONES

TIME: 30 MIN.

Practice Sequence 1:

15 minutes

The X1 player passes to X2 and makes a diagonal run between the cones.

X2 passes the ball to X1 outside of the cones and then makes a diagonal run outside the opposite cone.

Practice Sequence 2:

15 minutes

X1 receives a pass from the server and passes to X2. X2 runs to receive the pass, passes to X3 and makes a diagonal run to the outside.

X3 runs to receive the pass from X2 and attacks the goal.

The two defenders O1 and O2 threaten the attacking players as soon as the pass is played by the server.

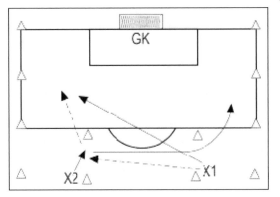

Practice Sequence 1

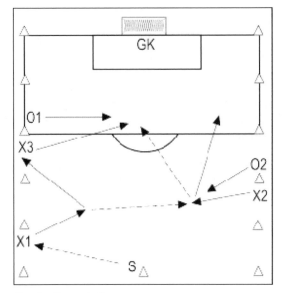

Practice Sequence 2

Attacking by crossing the ball

Layout:
Use the goal and penalty area of at least one half of a playing field.
The crossing lanes should be a minimum of 10 X 30 yards and if possible 10 X 40 yards.

The target area should be marked so that it can clearly be seen, and should be 20 X 8 yards extending 2 yards inside the goal area in line with the goal.

General:
Practice the crosses first, concentrating on accuracy into the target area.

When the crosses are good, continue with the attacking player sequence of one X player, then with the two attacking players and one defender.

The crosses should be executed before the end of the crossing lane.

Skills for attacking by crossing the ball

Crosses:
The crossing player should make a run with the ball in the crossing lane and, before the end of the lane, make a lofted pass into the target area.

Attacking players:
The first attacking player nearest the crossing player should make an angled run to the near post, making sure he is behind the ball until the ball is crossed.

The second attacking player should make an angled run to the far post, making sure he is behind the ball until the ball is crossed.

The attacking players should attack the ball and shoot on goal at the first opportunity.

KEY			
Ball Movement	⟶	Player Movement	------➤
Attacking Player	X	Defending Player	0
Server	S	Goalkeeper	GK

Key Factors:
1. The crosses should be played early into the target area.
2. The attacker nearest the ball should make a run for the near post.
3. The attacker furthest from the ball should make a run for the far post.
4. Attackers should keep behind the player crossing the ball.

EQUIPMENT: GOAL AND PENALTY AREA, RUNNING LANES, 10 BALLS, BIBS   **TIME: 30 MIN.**

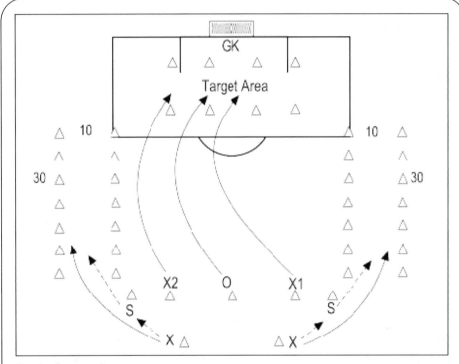

Practice Sequence 1

Practice Sequence 1:
10 minutes
The X player passes the ball to the server and runs into the running lane.
The server S returns the pass to X in the running lane.
X runs to the end of the running lane and makes a cross into the target area.

Practice Sequence 2:
10 minutes
The X1 player starts and makes an angled run to the near post, collecting the cross, keeping onside behind the player crossing the ball.

Practice Sequence 3:
10 minutes
The X2 player is added to the practice to make an angled run to the far post.
The O player is also added as a defender.

Attacking the ball around the goal

Layout:
Use an actual goal and penalty area and where possible to make the practice realistic.

The cones should be positioned at least 5 yards to the side of the penalty area to give enough space to make the throw or lofted pass.

General:
The X players should attempt a first time shot or header on the goal from the lofted pass or throw-in.

In the second practice add an extra attacker and 2 defenders, giving an advantage to the attacking players.

Encourage the players to try different techniques to score a goal.

Skills for attacking the ball around the goal

General:
The first choice of an attacking player in the penalty area is to accept the responsibility to shoot. Missing the target should not put players off from shooting again.

Players should not be afraid of a physical challenge and should be prepared to perform difficult techniques around the goal.

Attacking the ball around the goal:
Always be first to the ball.
Receive the ball, turn and shoot in one movement.
The player should move in one direction, check and move away from the opponent.
First time shooting around opponents.
Trap the ball and feint before shooting to unbalance the opponent.

KEY

Ball Movement	⟶		Player Movement	----➤
Attacking Player	X		Defending Player	0
Server	S		Goalkeeper	GK

Key Factors:

1. Be first to the ball.
2. Receive the ball and turn in one movement.
3. Control the ball and shoot around opponents.
4. Move in one direction, check and move away from the opponent.

EQUIPMENT: Goal and penalty area, 10 Balls, Bibs, Cones   TIME: 30 min.

Practice Sequence 1:

15 minutes

S1 makes a lofted pass into the penalty area alternating with S2 who makes a throw-in, into the penalty area, but not at the same time.

The 3 X players make an attacking play on the ball to score a goal.

Practice Sequence 2:

15 minutes

S1 makes a lofted pass into the penalty area alternating with S2 who makes a throw-in into the penalty area, but not at the same time.

The 4 X players make an attacking play on the ball to score a goal while the 2 O players defend the goal, supporting the goalkeeper

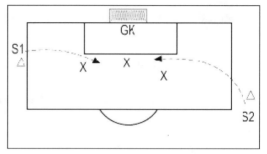

Practice Sequence 1

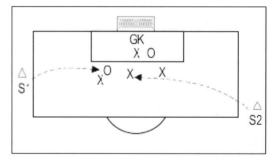

Practice Sequence 2

Attacking in and around the penalty area

Layout:
Use an actual goal and penalty area plus a grid outside the area, which should be 30 to 40 yards from the end line, stretching across the field.

General:
The attacking players X should create space for each other and shoot at the first good opportunity.

The ball is in play until it goes out of bounds or a goal is scored.

Skills for attacking in and around the penalty area

Creating space:
Running behind the defense.
Coming to the player with the ball.
Running wide or overlap running.

Player on the ball:
The player on the ball should keep his head up where possible and make the decision to shoot, pass or dribble.

As soon as the player with the ball has passed to another player, space should be created to receive the ball again.

General:
All players should be moving and creating space for the player on the ball.

KEY			
Ball Movement	→	Player Movement	- - - →
Attacking Player	X	Defending Player	0
Server	S	Goalkeeper	GK

Key Factors:
1. Create space.
2. Make an early decision to shoot, dribble or pass.
3. Attack the back of the defense.
4. Timing and accuracy of the passes.

EQUIPMENT: Goal and penalty area, 10 Balls, Bibs, Cones   TIME: 30 min.

Practice Sequence 1:

15 minutes

The goalkeeper passes the ball to X1. When X1 touches the ball the practice is live.

X2 and X3 join X1 in the attack while O1 and O2 defend the area.

Practice Sequence 2:

15 minutes

The goalkeeper throws the ball to X1. When X1 touches the ball, the practice is live.

X2, X3 and X4 join X1 in the attack while O1, O2 and O3 defend the area giving a 4 v 3 situation with the attackers having the numerical advantage.

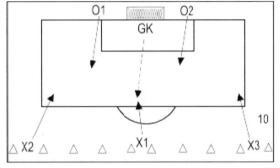

Practice Sequence 1

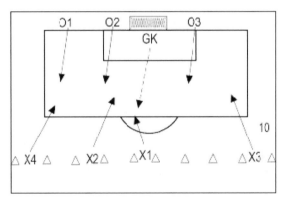

Practice Sequence 2

93

Passing back to the goalkeeper

Layout:
Use a goal and penalty area.

For practice 1 place the cones for the practicing players 10 yards from the penalty area and in line with the goal area.

For practice 2 add 2 cones each side 10 yards away.

General:
In practice sequence 1 start the practice with the goalkeeper throwing the ball out to the defending player. After the ball is passed from the goalkeeper back to the defender, the defending player should pass the ball to the next defender.

In practice sequence 2 switch starting the play to either side by the goalkeeper throwing the ball. The goalkeeper should make the decision which defender to pass the ball to.

Skills for passing back to the goalkeeper

Defending player:
Keep the ball close and run at a controlled speed, protecting the ball from the opponent.

Pass the ball back to the goalkeeper, to the area outside of the goal posts.

Run to a position at the side of the penalty area to receive the ball from the goalkeeper.

Goalkeeper:
The goalkeeper should bring the ball under control (not with hands) quickly and then kick the ball to the side line or to an unmarked defender. If the goalkeeper is under pressure from an opposing player, the ball must be cleared immediately.

KEY

Ball Movement	⟶	Player Movement	----→
Attacking Player	X	Defending Player	0
Server	S	Goalkeeper	GK

Key Factors:

1. Check the position of the goalkeeper.
2. Run back at a controlled speed.
3. Keep the ball within playing distance and away from the attacking player.
4. Move to a good position to receive the ball from the goalkeeper.

EQUIPMENT: Goal and penalty area, 10 Balls, Bibs, Cones | TIME: 30 min.

Practice Sequence 1:

10 minutes

The goalkeeper throws the ball out to the defender O who runs back towards the goalkeeper to return the ball.

The O defender then runs to the side of the penalty area to receive the returned pass from the goalkeeper.

The attacking player X should put pressure on the defender and try to prevent the goalkeeper from making a return pass.

Practice Sequence 2:

10 minutes

The goalkeeper throws the ball out to one of the defenders O1 or O2. Both run back towards the goalkeeper and the defender with the ball passes back to the goalkeeper.

Both the defenders run to the side of the penalty area to receive the returned pass from the goalkeeper.

The attacking players X1 and X2 should put pressure on the defenders to make a mistake.

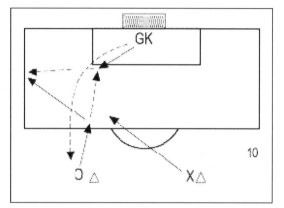

Practice Sequence 1

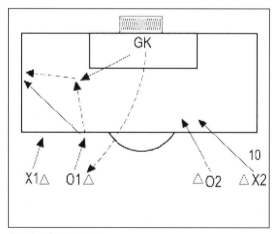

Practice Sequence 2

Goalkeeping corner kicks and crosses

Layout:
Use a goal and penalty area as well as the area at the corners and side lines. Place cones at 10 yards from the corners of the penalty area.

General:
Start the practice with 3 or 4 players taking corner kicks to the goalkeeper. Use actual corner positions for taking corner kicks.

The two defenders O1 and O2 should communicate with the goalkeeper and the two attackers X1 and X2 should try to score goals.

Switch the servers taking corner kicks if the corner kicks or the crosses are not of a good quality.

The crosses should be taken outside the penalty area at an angle of 10 yards from the corner of the penalty area.

Skills for goalkeeping corners and crosses

Starting position:
The position of the goalkeeper should allow an observation angle of 180 degrees. The body of the goalkeeper should be open and parallel with the goal line.

Attacking the ball:
Make an early decision based on the trajectory of the ball.

Move late to the ball to give more time to asses the trajectory of the ball, but move quickly and take the ball at its highest point.

Communicate with the defenders and inform them when to move and in which direction.

KEY

Ball Movement	⟶	Player Movement	------>
Attacking Player	X	Defending Player	0
Server	S	Goalkeeper	GK

Key Factors :
1. Goalkeeper starting position.
2. Decision to attack or stay and defend the goal.
3. Communications with defenders.
4. Timing and accuracy in attacking the ball.

EQUIPMENT: GOAL AND PENALTY AREA, 10 BALLS, BIBS, CONES   **TIME:** 30 MIN.

Practice Sequence 1:
10 minutes
The servers S1 and S2 take turns taking corner kicks into the penalty area.
O1 and O2 are defenders and should support the goalkeeper. X1 and X2 act as attackers to put pressure on the goalkeeper.

Practice Sequence 2:
10 minutes
The servers S1 and S2 take turns making crosses into the penalty area.
O1 and O2 are defenders and should support the goalkeeper. X1 and X2 act as attackers to put pressure on the goalkeeper.

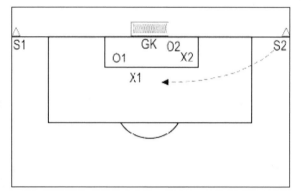

Practice Sequence 1

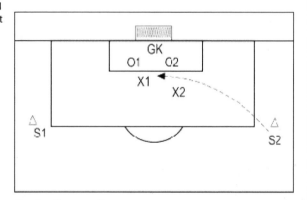

Practice Sequence 2

Goalkeeper: Narrowing the angle

Layout:
Use a goal and penalty area.

Place the cones for the practicing players 10 yards from the penalty area .

General:
The attacking player X should run at the goal as if he has broken clear of the defense.
The defender should put pressure on the attacker to prevent him from scoring.
In practice 2 the goalkeeper may throw the ball to either X1 or X2.
The practice commences when the attacker has the ball under control and moves towards the goal.

Skills for narrowing the angle by the goalkeeper

Starting position:
The goalkeeper should be at such a distance from the goal that he can get back to the goal line to intercept a lob from the attacking player. The goal-keeper should be in a position to attack the intervening space in front of the attacking player:

Approach and speed:
The approach of the goalkeeper to the ball should be between the center of the back of the goal and the ball. The goalkeeper should move as fast as pos-sible towards the ball when the ball is outside the playing distance of the attacking player.

Body stance and barrier:
The goalkeeper should stand up and create a large enough obstacle to deter the oncoming attacker. When the goalkeeper has made up enough ground to narrow the angle of the attacker he should go to the ground, spreading his body in a long barrier across the angle between the ball and the goal.

KEY			
Ball Movement	⟶	Player Movement	------➤
Attacking Player	X	Defending Player	0
Server	S	Goalkeeper	GK

Key Factors :
1. Starting position of the goalkeeper.
2. Angle of approach to the ball.
3. Speed of approach to the ball.
4. Body stance on the approach to the ball.

EQUIPMENT: GOAL AND PENALTY AREA, 10 BALLS, BIBS, CONES   **TIME:** 20 MIN.

Practice Sequence 1:

10 minutes

The goalkeeper throws the ball to the attacking player X who runs to score a goal.

The goalkeeper should reduce the angle of the attacker while O runs back to defend.

O can start when X has control of the ball.

Practice Sequence 2:

10 minutes

The goalkeeper throws the ball to one of the attacking players (X1 or X2) and both run to attack the goal.

The goalkeeper should reduce the angle of the attacker with the ball while O1 and O2 run back to defend.

The defenders O1 and O2 can start when the attacking player has control of the ball.

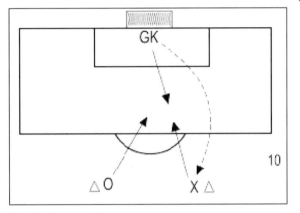

Practice Sequence 1

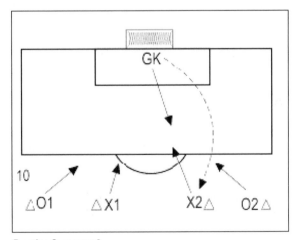

Practice Sequence 2

Ball possession

Layout:
Set up session 1 with the practice grids of 10 X 30 yards with 1 goal of 3 yards at one end.
Set up session 2 with the practice grids of 15 X 30 yards with a goal at each end of 3 yards each.
Set up session 3 with one practice grid of 20 X 40 yards with a goal at each end of 5 yards each.

General:
In sessions 2 and 3 make each player responsible for marking a specific player.

The grids are kept small to make possession more difficult, but if the players have difficulties increase the size of the grids.

Skills for ball possession

Passing to keep ball possession:
The pass should be accurate and the timing should be to maximize the position of the receiving player.

A variety of techniques should be used depending on the position of the receiving player.

The passing player should try to disguise where the pass is going.

Support:
The supporting player should arrive at the correct position at the right time to receive the ball.

The supporting player should be prepared to receive and control the ball in a crowded area and be ready to pass the ball to another team player.

Always be ready to receive a pass and get quickly into position.

KEY

Ball Movement	⟶		Player Movement	--------➤
Attacking Player	X		Defending Player	0
Server	S		Goalkeeper	GK

Key Factors:
1. Keep close control of the ball.
2. Shield the ball while looking for a team player to pass to.
3. Create space to receive the ball while not in ball possession.
4. Players communicating with each other and ready to receive the ball

EQUIPMENT: GRIDS CREATED FROM CONES, 10 BALLS, BIBS   TIME: 40 MIN.

Practice Sequence 1:
10 minutes
The server plays the ball to X1 or X2 who play to keep possession of the ball against defender O.
The X players should attempt to score a goal in the small goal at one end.

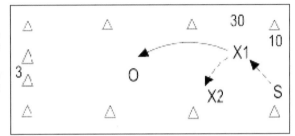

Practice Sequence 1

Practice Sequence 2:
10 minutes
This is a 3 v 3 situation where both teams try to keep possession of the ball and attempt to score a goal.
When the ball goes out of the grid, server 1 and server 2 alternate playing the next ball into the grid area.
Server 1 plays to the X players and server 2 to the O players.

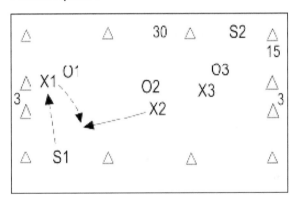

Practice Sequence 2

Practice Sequence 3:
20 minutes
This is a 6 v 6 situation where both teams try to keep possession of the ball and attempt to score a goal.
When the ball goes out of the grid, server 1 and server 2 alternate playing the next ball into the grid area.
Server 1 plays to the X players and server 2 to the O players.

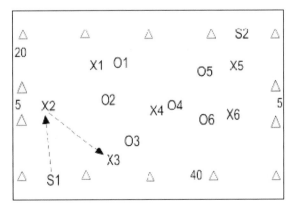

Practice Sequence 3

Creating space by passing inside

Layout:
This practice should be set up using a goal and penalty area.
For practice 1 place cones 30 yards from the end line.
For practice 2 place cones 40 yards from the end line.

General:
The sequence can take place starting from the left and then from the right and then alternate.
The defenders in practice 2 should not start before the attacker but must threaten the play.

Skills for creating space by passing inside

Passing:
The pace on the ball must be with enough pace to reach its target but not so strong that it is difficult to control.

The timing of the pass should be to maximize the position of the player receiving the pass and place the opponents at a disadvantage.

Running:
The player should make a controlled run, always expecting the ball to be passed.

The run should be into space created by the player who passed the ball.

KEY

Ball Movement	⟶		Player Movement	----⟶
Attacking Player	X		Defending Player	0
Server	S		Goalkeeper	GK

Key Factors:

1. Timing and accuracy of the pass.
2. Timing and accuracy of the runs.
3. Run to the inside of the player with the ball.
4. Receive the ball with body between opponent and the ball.

EQUIPMENT: GOAL AND PENALTY AREA, 10 BALLS, BIBS   **TIME:** 30 MIN.

Practice Sequence 1:

15 minutes

The server passes the ball to X1.
X2 runs to collect the pass from X1.

X2 then makes a run to score a goal. X1 runs forward to create space for X2.

Practice right and left.

Practice Sequence 2:

15 minutes

X2 runs to collect the pass from the server.

X1 runs to collect the pass from X2.

X2 runs into the penalty area to collect the return pass from X1.

X2 makes a strike on goal while X1 creates space in the penalty area.

Practice right and left.

The O defenders should try to prevent the passes.

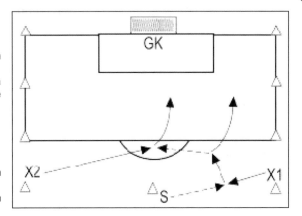

Practice Sequence 1

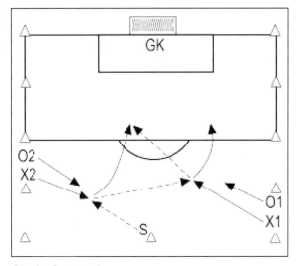

Practice Sequence 2

Defending against opponents facing the goal

Layout:
This practice should be set up using a goal and penalty area
In practice 1 use the penalty area but place cones at 10 yards from the penalty area where the players should start.
In practice 2 set cones at 30 yards from the end line.

General:
In practice 1 the defender O should defend against the attacker inside the penalty area but the attacker should attempt to score a goal.

In practice 2 the two defenders should defend the grid area from the two attackers.

If the ball goes out of the grid the sequence is finished and the next defenders and attackers should start.

Skills for defending against opponents facing the goal

Defending:
The defending player should watch the ball when in a challenging position.

It is important for the defending player to adopt the ideal position, which is between 1 to 1.5 yards from the attacker.

The defender should be patient and concentrate on when to select the correct moment to tackle. The best moment is when the attacker attempts to turn.

Supporting:
The supporting player should be positioned at an angle behind the defender, in line with where the attacker is being steered.

The supporting player should communicate with the defender.

KEY

Ball Movement	→	Player Movement	- - - ->	
Attacking Player	X	Defending Player	0	
Server	S	Goalkeeper	GK	

Key Factors:

1. Close the space down quickly between defender and attacker.
2. Make a curved run to show direction to steer opponent.
3. Shuffle last 2 steps with the leading foot outside of the line of the ball.
4. Supporting player angle and position.

EQUIPMENT: GOAL AND PENALTY AREA, 10 BALLS, BIBS, CONES   **TIME:** 30 MIN.

Practice Sequence 1:

15 minutes

The X player passes the ball to the server who passes between the X player and the defender O.

The X player should receive the ball first and should attempt to score a goal.

Alternate the play both right and left.

Practice Sequence 2:

15 minutes

The X2 player passes the ball to the server who returns the pass.

X2 controls the ball and dribbles towards the goal.

The O2 player defends against the X2 player.

O1 supports O2 but tracks the position of X1 who also attacks.

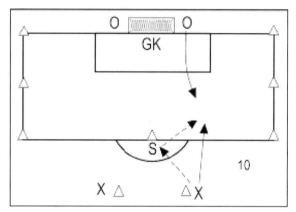

Practice Sequence 1

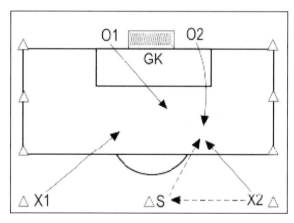

Practice Sequence 2

Defending and support in the penalty area

Layout:
For practice 1, create a grid of 15 X 10 yards with an 8 yard goal marked with cones at one end and use 4 players plus a goalkeeper and 2 servers to each grid.
For practice 2 and 3 use an actual goal and penalty area.

General:
In practice 1 the defenders should start the sequence in the middle of the grid and the attackers should attempt to score a goal.

In practices 2 and 3 the defenders should start the sequence in the middle of the penalty area and give space for the attacking players.

If the ball goes out of the grid, the sequence is finished and the next set of defenders and attackers should start.

Skills for defending and support in the penalty area

Defending:
The defending player should watch the ball when in a challenging position.

It is important for the defending player to adopt the ideal position which is between 1 to 1.5 yards from the attacker.

The defender should be patient and concentrate on selecting the correct moment to tackle, the best moment being when the attacker attempts to turn.

Supporting player:
The supporting player should be positioned at an angle behind the defender, where the attacker is being sent.

The supporting player should communicate with the defender.

KEY

Ball Movement	⟶		Player Movement	---------➤
Attacking Player	X		Defending Player	0
Server	S		Goalkeeper	GK

Key Factors:
1. Travel quickly when the ball is played to the opponent to be defended.
2. Slow down when closing in on the opponent.
3. Prevent the ball from being played forward.
4. Recover defensive position when the ball is played.

EQUIPMENT: Goal and penalty area, 10 Balls, Bibs, Cones | TIME: 30 min.

Practice Sequence 1:
10 minutes
The server passes the ball to the X player on the opposite side of the grid.
The 2 X players should play the ball between them and attempt to score a goal.
The O defenders should start the sequence in the middle of the grid and defend the goal.
Alternate the starting between servers.

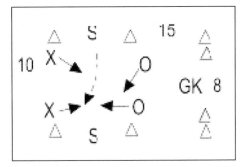

Practice Sequence 1

Practice Sequence 2:
10 minutes
To start either server S1 passes the ball to X1 or server S2 passes to X2.
The 2 O players defend against the X players to prevent a goal from being scored.
The sequence stops when the ball goes out of the penalty area

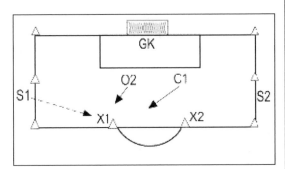

Practice Sequence 2

Practice Sequence 3:
10 minutes
Start with either server S1 passing the ball to X1 or server S2 passing to X2.
The O players defend against the X players to prevent a goal from being scored.
The sequence stops when the ball goes out of the penalty area.

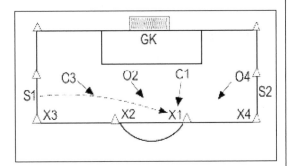

Practice Sequence 3

Defending with a sweeper

Layout:
In this practice use a goal and penalty area with cones placed 30 yards from the end line to create a grid.

General:
Keep a close watch on both the two defenders and the sweeper positioning.

In practice 1 the ball can be played directly from one side to the other side of the penalty area.

In practice 2 if the ball goes out of the grid, the sequence is finished and the next defenders and attackers should start.

Skills for defending with a sweeper

Sweeper positioning:
Always keep goal side of the opponent and occupy space, moving around the penalty spot behind or ahead of the defense.

Keep all opponents and the ball in view, especially on the opposite side to where the ball is.

Sweeper Responsibilities:
Mark the unmarked player inside or outside shooting distance.

Defend against an unmarked player with the ball attacking the goal or making a pass into the penalty area.

Positioning and communicating with the team.

KEY

Ball Movement	⟶		Player Movement	- - - - ⟶
Attacking Player	X		Defending Player	0
Server	S		Goalkeeper	GK

Key Factors:
1. Sweeper position around the penalty spot.
2. Communicating with the defense.
3. Keep the ball and all players in view.
4. Defend the unmarked player.

EQUIPMENT: GOAL AND PENALTY AREA, 10 BALLS, BIBS, CONES

TIME: 30 MIN.

Practice Sequence 1:
10 minutes

The X players pass the ball to each other while the sweeper and goalkeeper move into position.

The sweeper should always be aware of what is happening on both sides of the field.

When one of the X players does not have the ball he should move to another position.

Practice Sequence 2:
20 minutes

X3 passes the ball to X1 or X2 and all 3 X players attack the goal.

O1 and O2 defend while the sweeper defends behind the marking players.

Either X1 or X2 should move to the blind side of the sweeper.

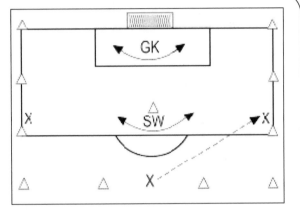

Practice Sequence 1

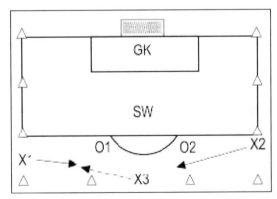

Practice Sequence 2

Running at angles

Layout:
In practice 1 make a 10 X 40 yards grid with a series of cones down the middle at 5 yards apart from each other.

In practices 2 and 3 the grid should be the width of the penalty area and 30 yards from the end line.

General:
In practice 1 if the players lose control of the ball they should run out of the grid and the next players should start the sequence.

In practices 2 and 3 if the ball goes out of the grid the sequence is finished and the next defenders and attackers should start.

Skills for running at angles

Running:
The players should run into space where the ball should be played and collect the ball.

Ground passing:
The foot is turned outward so that the inside of the boot makes contact with the ball at right angles to the line of the pass.

To keep the ball low, the contact of the boot on the ball should be through the horizontal mid-line of the ball, with the body over the ball.

The position of the head should be steady with eyes looking down at the ball while passing.

KEY

Ball Movement	⟶		Player Movement	------→
Attacking Player	X		Defending Player	0
Server	S		Goalkeeper	GK

Key Factors:
1. Timing and accuracy of the passes and the pace on the ball.
2. Timing and angle of the runs.
3. Run quickly but at a controlled speed.
4. Create space away from the opponent to receive and pass the ball.

EQUIPMENT: Goal and penalty area, 10 Balls, Bibs, Cones | TIME: 30 MIN.

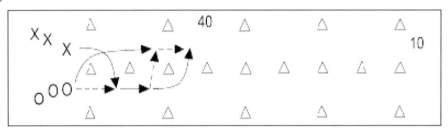

Practice Sequence 1:
10 minutes

O passes the ball directly along the line of the cones for X to run through the cones onto the ball. O then runs around to the opposite side of the cones to receive a return pass through the cones. O plays the ball along the line of cones and X plays the ball through the cones.

Practice Sequence 2:
10 minutes

The server plays the ball into the path of X1 to run onto.

X1 runs with the ball to the middle of the penalty area and passes to X2.

X1 makes a diagonal run while X2 controls the ball and passes it into the path of X1.

X2 makes a run into the middle of the penalty area to receive the return pass from X1 to shoot on goal.

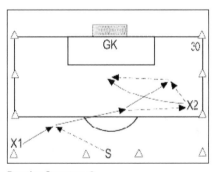

Practice Sequence 2

Practice Sequence 3:
10 minutes

The server plays the ball into the path of X1 to run onto.

X1 runs with the ball to the middle of the penalty area and passes to X2.

X1 makes a diagonal run while X2 controls the ball and passes it into the path of X1.

X2 makes a run into the middle of the penalty area to receive the return pass from X1 to shoot on goal.

O1 and O2 must prevent the X players from scoring a goal.

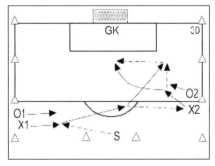

Practice Sequence 3

Finishing from crosses

Layout:
In this practice use a goal and penalty area with cones placed 30 yards from the end line to create a grid.

General:
Make sure the players in the penalty area move away from the goal to create more space at the start of each sequence.

The attacking players should attempt a first time shot or header on goal from the cross.

In the second practice add 1 extra attacker and 2 defenders, giving an advantage to the attacking players.

Skills for finishing from crosses

Creating space:
The attacking player should move away from the ball and when the crossing player's head goes down to make the cross, then move in front of the defending player.

Attacking crosses:
Players should not be afraid of a physical challenge and should be prepared to perform difficult techniques around the goal.

Missing the target should not put players off from shooting again.

Different techniques should be encouraged:
- Receiving the ball and turning in one movement
- Shooting around opponents
- Feinting before shooting to unbalance the opponent.
- Direct shot on goal.

KEY

Ball Movement	⟶		Player Movement	------➤
Attacking Player	X		Defending Player	0
Server	S		Goalkeeper	GK

Key Factors:

1. Create space by moving in the opposite direction to the crossing player.
2. Attack when the crossing player's head goes down to cross the ball.
3. Move in front of opponents as the cross comes in.
4. Be first and attack the ball.

EQUIPMENT: GOAL AND PENALTY AREA, 10 BALLS, BIBS, CONES   **TIME: 30 MIN.**

Practice Sequence 1:

15 minutes

X1 passes to the server and runs to receive the returned pass, controls the ball and makes a cross into the penalty area.

The attacking X players attempt to make a first time shot on goal.

Use both X1 and X2 to create left and right crosses.

Practice Sequence 2:

15 minutes

X1 passes to the server and runs to receive the returned pass, controls the ball and makes a cross into the penalty area.

The attacking X players attempt to make a first time shot on goal.

Use both X1 and X2 to create left and right crosses.

The 2 0 defenders should protect the goal and defend realistically.

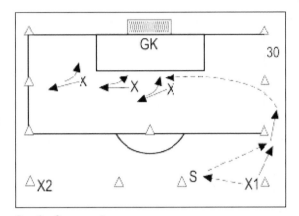

Practice Sequence 1

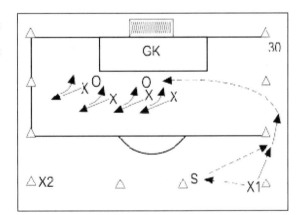

Practice Sequence 2

Creating space in attack

Layout:
Use an actual goal and penalty area plus an outside grid area.

The grid for practice 1 should be 30 yards from the end line.

The grid for practice 2 should be 40 yards from the end line.

General:
If the ball goes out of the grid area the practice should start again.

The players should create space as soon as the ball is played.

Skills for creating space in attack

Creating Space:
Running behind the defense
Coming to the player with the ball
Running wide or overlap running

General:
All players should be moving either with the ball or creating space to receive the ball.

KEY

Ball Movement	⟶		Player Movement	⇢
Attacking Player	X		Defending Player	0
Server	S		Goalkeeper	GK

Key Factors:
1. Create space to receive the ball.
2. Play the ball behind the defense and into the path of the receiving player.
3. Control the ball quickly and pass or make a one touch pass.
4. Always be prepared to receive the ball and be aware of the defense.

EQUIPMENT: GOAL AND PENALTY AREA, 10 BALLS, BIBS, CONES　　　TIME: 30 MIN.

Practice Sequence 1:
15 minutes
X3 runs to receive the ball from the server and then plays to X2 who comes to collect the ball.
X2 plays the ball into the path of X1 who makes a diagonal run to collect the ball.
X3 makes a run through the middle of the penalty area.
X1 should shoot to score a goal or pass to X3.
Alternate the starting point left and right.

Practice Sequence 2:
15 minutes
X3 runs to receive the ball from the server and then plays to X2 who comes to collect the ball.
X2 can play the ball into the path of X1 or into the path of X3.
X1 or X3 should shoot to score a goal if possible or pass the ball off.
Both the defenders O1 and O2 should try to prevent the attackers from passing and scoring a goal.
Alternate the starting point left and right.

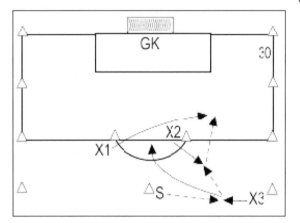

Practice Sequence 1

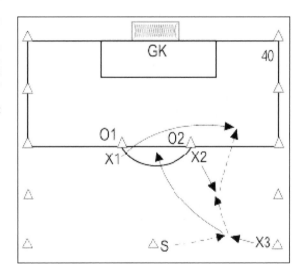

Practice Sequence 2

115

Crossing from the end line

Layout:
Use an actual goal and penalty area plus an outside grid.
The target area should be marked so that it can clearly be seen, and should be 20 X 8 yards extending 2 yards inside the goal area in line with the goal.
In practice 1 set up the outside cones at 30 yards from the end line.
In practice 2 set up 2 sets of cones at 30 and 40 yards from the end line.

General:
In practice 1 concentrate on the crosses and make sure the crosses are played into the target area.
In practice 2 work with the players and ensure they arrive in the area at the correct time to attack the ball.

Techniques and skills for crossing and attacking the ball

Crossing the ball:
The crossing player should make a controlled run with the ball, kicking it with the outside of the foot.

Between kicking the ball the crossing player should keep the head up to assess the position of the players.

The cross can be a ground pass to the near post or lofted pass to the far post but into the target area.

Attacking crosses:
The attacking players should make an angled run so as to be facing the ball when it is delivered.

The time to attack is when the crossing player's head goes down to cross the ball.

The attacking player should take the first opportunity to get in front of the defense and play the ball first time.

KEY

Ball Movement	⟶	Player Movement	------>
Attacking Player	X	Defending Player	0
Server	S	Goalkeeper	GK

Key Factors:
1. Run at controlled speed to the end line, keeping the ball under control.
2. Cross the ball into the target area using a ground, chip or lofted pass.
3. Attacking players should make angled runs into target area.
4. Attacking players should arrive in the penalty area facing the ball.

EQUIPMENT: GOAL AND PENALTY AREA, 10 BALLS, BIBS, CONES   **TIME:** 30 MIN.

Practice Sequence 1:

15 minutes

X1 passes the ball to the sever who passes the ball back to X1.
X1 makes a controlled run with the ball to the end line and crosses the ball into the target area.
X2 makes an angled run into the target area.

Practice Sequence 2:

15 minutes

X1 passes the ball to the server who passes the ball to X2.
X2 then passes the ball to X1 who makes an overlap run to the end line to make a cross into the target area.
X2 and X3 make angled runs into the target area.
Both O1 and O2 should defend realistically.

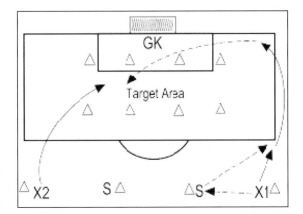

Practice Sequence 1

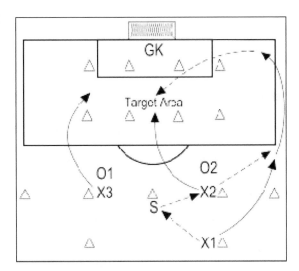

Practice Sequence 2

117

Crossing from the side of the penalty area

Layout:
Use the goal and penalty area and at least one half of a soccer field.

The side goal target areas should be 10 X 3 yards and 2 yards from the end line, and placed at both sides of the goal area line.

In practice 1 the starting cones should be a 5 yard triangle placed 30 yards from the end line.
In practice 2 place the starting cones at 40 yards from the end line.

General:
In practice 1 concentrate on the crosses and make sure the crosses are played into the target areas either to the near post or to the far post.
In practice 2 work with the players to ensure they arrive in the target areas at the correct time.

Techniques and skills for crossing the ball

Crossing the ball:
The crossing player should make a controlled run, kicking the ball with the outside of the foot.

Between kicking the ball, the crossing player should keep the head up to assess the position of the players.

The cross can be a ground pass to the near post or lofted pass to the far post but into the target area.

Attacking crosses:
The attacking players should make an angled run so as to be facing the ball when it is delivered.

The time to attack is when the crossing player's head goes down to cross the ball.

The attacking players should take the first opportunity to get in front of the defense and play the ball first time.

KEY

Ball Movement	⟶		Player Movement	----------➤
Attacking Player	X		Defending Player	0
Server	S		Goalkeeper	GK

Key Factors:

1. Run with the ball at controlled speed.
2. A lofted pass or ground pass to the opposite side of the goal area.
3. Accuracy and timing of the cross.
4. Attacking players should make an angled run into the penalty area.

EQUIPMENT: Goal and penalty area, 10 Balls, Bibs, Cones   **TIME:** 30 min.

Practice Sequence 1:

15 minutes

X plays the ball to the server who returns the pass into the path of the X player.

X collects the pass and controls the ball for a cross into the target area on the opposite side of the goal area.

The cross is delivered outside the penalty area.

Practice with both right and left crosses.

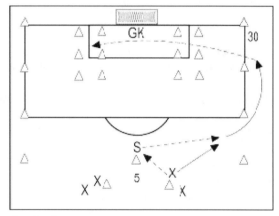

Practice Sequence 1

Practice Sequence 2:

15 minutes

X1 plays the ball to X3 who returns the pass into the path of X1.

X1 collects the pass, controls the ball and runs outside the penalty area for a cross into the target zone on the opposite side of the goal area.

X2 and X3 make angled runs into the target area.

O1 and O2 defend against X1 and X2.

Practice with both right and left crosses.

Practice Sequence 2

Attacking inside the penalty area

Layout:
This practice should be set up using an actual goal and penalty area

The grid for practices 1 and 2 should be the middle 20 yards of the penalty area.
For practice 3 use the whole of the penalty area.

General:
The practice should be as realistic as possible in the confines of the grid area. If the ball goes out of the grid another ball should be played by the server.

Switch players around to give all players the opportunity to practice.

Techniques and skills for attacking inside the penalty area

Attacking player:
The first choice of an attacking player is to accept the responsibility to get in front of the defender and shoot when possible or pass the ball.

Players should not be afraid of a physical challenge and should be prepared to perform difficult techniques around the goal.

Different techniques should be encouraged:
- Receiving the ball and turning in one movement
- Moving in one direction and checking and moving away from the opponent
- Shooting around opponents
- Feinting before shooting to unbalance the opponent.

Support Player:
Create space by moving away from the other attacker or behind the defensive player.

KEY

Ball Movement	⟶		Player Movement	- - - - - -⟶
Attacking Player	X		Defending Player	0
Server	S		Goalkeeper	GK

Key Factors:
1. Create space to receive the ball.
2. Turn and receive the ball in one move and shoot at first opportunity.
3. Get in front of the defender and be first to the ball.
4. Supporting player runs to create space to receive the ball.

EQUIPMENT: GOAL AND PENALTY AREA, 10 BALLS, BIBS, CONES   **TIME:** 30 MIN.

Practice Sequence 1:
10 minutes
Number the servers 1 through 3.
The X player calls a server's number and runs to collect the ball.
The X player has only two touches of the ball to bring it under control and shoot.
Change out X players after 6 consecutive balls.

Practice Sequence 2:
10 minutes
Number the servers 1 through 3.
The X player calls a server's number and runs to collect the ball.
The defender should prevent X from scoring a goal.
Change out X players after 6 consecutive balls.

Practice Sequence 3:
10 minutes
The servers S1 and S2 should alternately put the ball into play.
The servers can play the ball anywhere inside the penalty area.
X1 and X2 should run to receive the ball and score against defenders O1 and O2.

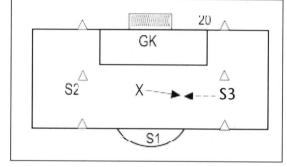

Practice Sequence 1

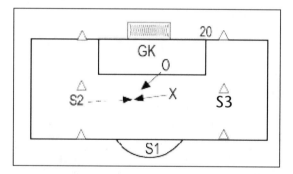

Practice Sequence 2

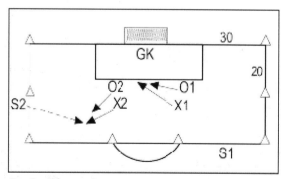

Practice Sequence 3

121

Attacking across the penalty area

Layout:
For this practice use an actual goal and penalty area.

The grid for practice 1 should be 10 X 15 yards with an 8 yard goal at one end.
For practices 2 and 3 use the whole of the penalty area.

General:
The practice should be as realistic as possible in the confines of the grid area. If the ball goes out of the grid another ball should be played by the server.

Switch players around to give all players the opportunity to practice.

Skills for attacking across the penalty area

Passing:
The passes should be played to an oncoming player or into space behind a defender for the attacking player to run onto.

The receiving player should control the ball quickly to have enough time to decide what is the next move.

Attacking player:
The first choice of an attacking player is to accept the responsibility to get in front of the defender and shoot when possible or pass the ball.

Players should not be afraid of a physical challenge and should be prepared to perform difficult techniques around the goal.

KEY

Ball Movement	⟶		Player Movement	- - - - -▶
Attacking Player	X		Defending Player	0
Server	S		Goalkeeper	GK

Key Factors:
1. Run to the end line and pass back across the penalty area.
2. Attacking players make curved runs across the goal.
3. Timing of the pass and run across the penalty area.
4. Be first to the ball and get in front of the defense.

EQUIPMENT: GOAL AND PENALTY AREA, 10 BALLS, BIBS, CONES

TIME: 30 MIN.

Practice Sequence 1:

10 minutes

X1 passes to X2 and runs outside the cones towards the end of the grid to receive the return pass from X2.

X1 runs with the ball to the end of the grid and passes the ball back to X2 who has run into position to receive the pass and shoot.

Alternate starting with X1 and X2.

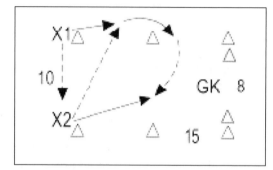

Practice Sequence 2:

10 minutes

X1 passes to X2 and runs outside the cones towards the end line to receive the return pass from X2.

X1 runs with the ball to the end line and passes the ball back across the penalty area for X2 or X3 to attack the goal.

Alternate starting left and right side of the penalty area.

Practice Sequence 1

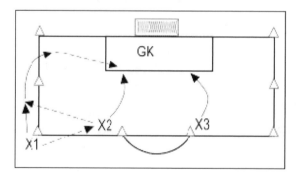

Practice Sequence 2

Practice Sequence 3:

10 minutes

X1 passes to X2 and runs outside the cones towards the end line to receive the return pass from X2.

X1 runs with the ball to the end line and passes the ball back across the penalty area for X2 or X3 to attack the goal.

O1 and O2 should defend the goal.

Alternate starting left and right side of the penalty area.

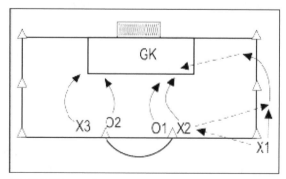

Practice Sequence 3

123

Running and passing at close angles

Layout:
For practice 1 set out the cones 5 yards apart, 5 yards across and 40 yards in length.

Practice 2 and 3 use the whole of the penalty area.

General:
In practice 1 keep the players moving by returning to the start after finishing the grid course but running well outside the grid area to allow the next players to practice.

In practices 2 and 3 keep to ground passing only and encourage quick delivery of the ball.
If the ball goes out of the grid start again with another group of players.
In practice 3 the defenders O should prevent the attackers from scoring.

Skills for running and passing at close angles

Passing:
Use quick and direct ground passes.
The passes should be played to an oncoming player or into the path of the attacking player to run onto.

The receiving player should control the ball quickly to give time to decide what the next move is and if possible, only use one touch.

Running:
The players should create space by running towards the player with the ball or by running away from a defender, creating space to receive the ball.

KEY				
Ball Movement	⟶		Player Movement	┈┈┈➤
Attacking Player	X		Defending Player	0
Server	S		Goalkeeper	GK

Key Factors:
1. Control the ball with first touch, a ground pass with the second touch.
2. Pass the ball into space in front of the receiving player.
3. Accuracy and timing of the pass.
4. The body should be over the ball and played with pace.

EQUIPMENT: GOAL AND PENALTY AREA, 10 BALLS, BIBS, CONES   TIME: 30 MIN.

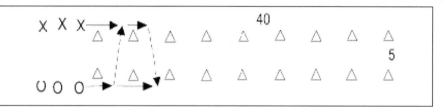

Practice Sequence 1:
10 minutes

The O and X players run along the outside of the cones and make diagonal passes across the grid. When the players reach the end of the grid they run back outside the grid with the ball to the beginning.

Practice Sequence 2:
10 minutes

The server makes a pass to X1 who controls the ball and passes immediately to the oncoming X2 player.

X3 makes a run into the middle of the penalty area to receive the direct pass from X2.

X3 should take a direct shot on goal.

Alternate starting left and right.

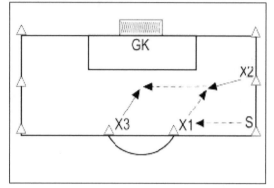

Practice Sequence 2

Practice Sequence 3:
10 minutes

The server makes a pass to X1 who controls the ball and passes immediately to the oncoming X2 player.

X3 makes a run into the middle of the penalty area to receive the direct pass from X2.

X3 can make a direct shot on goal or pass to X1 who has made an overlap run behind the defense.

Alternate starting left and right.

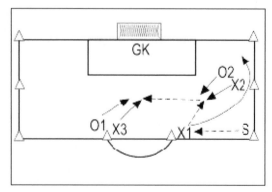

Practice Sequence 3

Dribbling in attack

Layout:
For practice 1 make the grid 15 X 15 yards with at least 6 additional cones as obstacles inside the grid.

In practice 2 use the goal and penalty area and set up cones from the goal line to the edge of the penalty area, and the width of the goal area. Place 5 cones inside the grid for the defending players.

In practice 3 use the whole of the penalty area.

General:
In practice 1 keep the players moving and use 2 groups of 4 players for each grid.

In practice 2 the defending players must touch their cone with one foot at all times but should try to tackle the ball with the other foot.

In practice 2 and 3 if the ball goes out of the grid start again.

Techniques and skills for dribbling

The approach:
The player should run at controlled speed directly at the opponent.

Feint and Dummy:
The dribbling player should unbalance the opponent by changing direction and or pace outside the tackling distance. Combining a feint with a change in direction can unbalance an opponent.

Explode into Space:
After unbalancing the opponent the dribbling player should explode into space behind the opponent.

KEY

Ball Movement	⟶	Player Movement	- - - - -⟶
Attacking Player	X	Defending Player	0
Server	S	Goalkeeper	GK

Key Factors:
1. Close control of the ball at all times.
2. Run at a controlled speed directly at the opponent.
3. Fake out the opponent, run quickly into the space created behind the opponent.
4. Keep good body balance.

EQUIPMENT: Goal and penalty area, 10 Balls, Bibs, Cones   **TIME:** 30 min.

Practice Sequence 1:

10 minutes

Players from both the X and O teams take turns dribbling around and through the cones and passing the ball to the next player.

Players from the X and O teams should dribble at the same time to be an obstruction to each other.

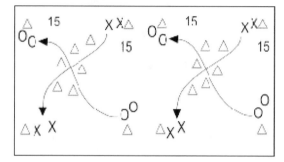

Practice Sequence 1

Practice Sequence 2:

10 minutes

The X player passes the ball to the server and runs into the grid area to receive the returned pass.

The X player then proceeds to dribble through the cones and the O players for a shot on goal.

The 5 O defenders must keep one foot on the cone but can use the other foot to defend the area.

Alternating starting left and right.

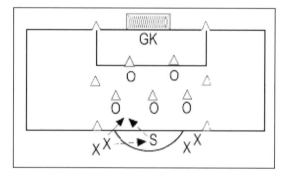

Practice Sequence 2

Practice Sequence 3:

10 minutes

The 3 O defending players should prevent an X player from scoring a goal.

The X players pass the ball around until one of the players has enough space to dribble towards the goal to take a shot.

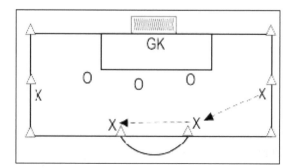

Practice Sequence 3

Goalkeeper distributing by throwing the ball

Layout:
For this practice set up a grid 20 X 30 yards with goals at each end.

General:
In practice 1 use only the 2 goalkeepers.

In practice 2 add 3 players for each team, 1 attacker and 2 defenders.

Skills and techniques for throwing the ball by the goalkeeper

Underarm throws:
The ball is released from a crouching position with a smooth underarm swing.

Over arm throws:
The body is in line with the direction of the throw and with weight on the back foot.
The ball is thrown as a straight arm bowling action. The ball is released at the top of the swing as the body weight moves to the front foot.

Javelin throws:
The body is in line with the direction of the throw and the ball is held as a javelin with a bent arm. The ball is released at the top of the arm swing with the arm following through.

KEY

Ball Movement	⟶		Player Movement	----➤
Attacking Player	X		Defending Player	0
Server	S		Goalkeeper	GK

Key Factors:
1. Selection of throwing techniques.
2. Accuracy and pace of the throw.
3. Communicating with team players.
4. Selection of when and where to begin the attack

EQUIPMENT: 2 GOALS AND GRID 20 X 30, 10 BALLS, BIBS   TIME: 20 MIN.

Practice Sequence 1:
10 minutes
The goalkeepers throw the ball to each other.
Concentrate on the 3 different throwing techniques:
Underarm throw.
Over arm throw.
Javelin throw.

Practice Sequence 2:
10 minutes
The goalkeepers throw the ball to one of the their players who play to shoot at the opposing goal.
The field players should move around giving different opportunities to receive the throw.
Keep the practice flowing by having enough balls available.
The field players should play realistically.

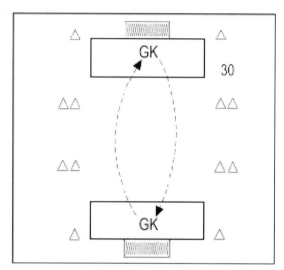

Practice Sequence 1

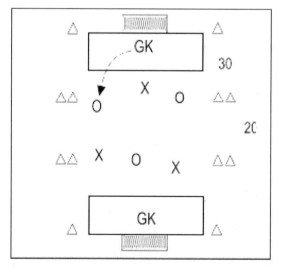

Practice Sequence 2

Creating space

General:
Set up a small sided game marked with cones at 60 X 40 yards with 2 full size goals, and cones marking the different thirds of the playing field.

Use 12 players plus 2 goalkeepers and coach only one unit of 6 players and a goalkeeper at one time.

Specific:
A two touch restriction in mid-field and attack should increase the range of vision and speed of decision on the ball.

It is also useful to reduce all players to a one touch restriction on the ball, but this will depend on the ability of the players.

Skills for creating space

Passing:
The passes should be played accurately to an oncoming player or into space behind a defender for the attacking player to run onto. If timed correctly, this will maximize the position of the player receiving the pass and place the opponent at a disadvantage.

The receiving player should control the ball quickly, if possible with one touch. This will give the player time to decide what is the next move and increase the range of vision.

Running:
The players should create space by running towards the player with the ball or running into the space behind the opponent.

The player who has just passed the ball should make a decision to move or to stand still.

KEY

Ball Movement	⟶		Player Movement	┄┄┄►
Attacking Player	X		Defending Player	0
Server	S		Goalkeeper	GK

Key Factors:
1. Head up to view the play.
2. Run to the ball or into space away from or behind an opponent.
3. Timing and accuracy of the pass.
4. Speed of decisions.

EQUIPMENT: SMALL SIDED FIELD 60 x 40 YARDS 10 BALLS, BIBS, CONES

TIME: 20 MIN.

Starting Position:
X2 starts with the ball and make a pass to O6. O6 then kicks the ball to the goalkeeper. The goalkeeper throws the ball to X1.
Switch the start point between X1/O5/X2 and X2/O6/X1.

Practice Sequence:
When O5 has kicked the ball to the goalkeeper the practice is live.
The goalkeeper throws the ball to either X1 or X2 who should have created enough space to receive the ball.
All other X players should be prepared to receive the ball.

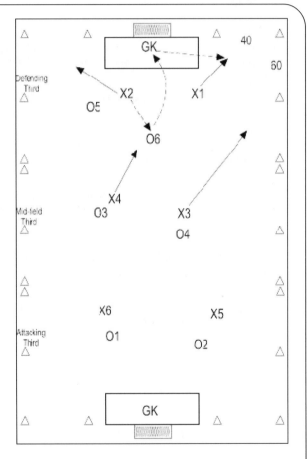

Overlap runs

General:
Set up a small sided game marked with cones at 60 X 40 yards with 2 full size goals and cones marking the different thirds of the playing field.

Use 12 players plus 2 goalkeepers and coach only one unit of 6 players and a goalkeeper at one time.

Specific:
The players should not be restricted to where they are playing on the field and overlap runs should be encouraged when and wherever possible.

Skills for overlap runs

Passing:
The pace on the ball must be fast enough to reach the target but not so strong that it is difficult to control.

The timing of the pass should optimize the position of the player receiving the pass and place the opponents at a disadvantage.

Running:
The player should make a controlled run outside of the player who was passed the ball, and always expect a return pass.

The run should be into space created by the player who was passed the ball and behind the opponent.

KEY			
Ball Movement	⟶	Player Movement	⇢
Attacking Player	X	Defending Player	0
Server	S	Goalkeeper	GK

Key Factors:

1. Run outside the player who was passed the ball.
2. Player communication.
3. Timing of the pass.
4. Run behind the opponent to create space.

EQUIPMENT: SMALL SIDED FIELD 60 x 40 YARDS, 10 BALLS, BIBS, CONES

TIME: 20 MIN.

Starting Position:

X2 starts with the ball and makes a pass to O6. O6 then kicks the ball to the goalkeeper. The goalkeeper throws the ball to X2.

Switch the start point between X1/O5 and X2/O6.

Practice Sequence:

When O6 has kicked the ball to the goalkeeper the practice is live.

The goalkeeper throws the ball to X2 who should have created enough space to receive the ball. X2 passes to X1 and makes an overlap run. All other X players should be prepared to receive the ball.

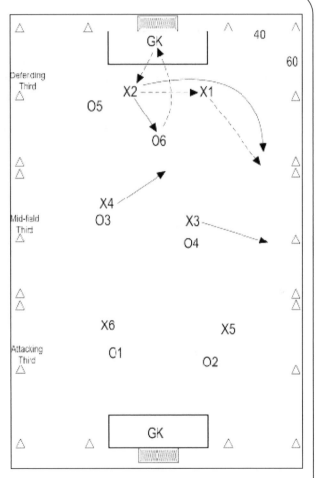

133

Diagonal running

General:
Set up a small sided game marked with cones at 60 X 40 yards with 2 full size goals and cones marking the different thirds of the playing field.

Use 12 players plus 2 goalkeepers and coach only one unit of 6 players and a goalkeeper at one time.

Specific:
A two touch ball restriction should increase the range of vision, speed of decision and speed of the ball.

Encourage the players to run diagonally across the field. For example, when a player comes to receive the ball, another player makes a diagonal run into the space vacated by that player.

Skills for diagonal runs

Passing:
The pass should be played to an oncoming player or into space behind a defender, for the attacking player to run onto.

The receiving player should control the ball quickly, and if possible with one touch of the ball. This will give the player more time to decide what is the next move.

The timing and accuracy of the pass should create space for the receiving player.

Running:
The players should create space by running towards the player with the ball or by running into space behind the defense.

The runs should always be made diagonally across the field.

KEY			
Ball Movement	⟶	Player Movement	- - - - -➤
Attacking Player	X	Defending Player	0
Server	S	Goalkeeper	GK

Key Factors:
1. Timing and accuracy of the pass and the pace on the ball.
2. Timing and angle of the runs.
3. Runs should be made diagonally across the field.
4. Create space by running towards the ball or behind an opponent.

EQUIPMENT: SMALL SIDED FIELD 60 x 40 YARDS, 10 BALLS, BIBS   **TIME:** 20 MIN.

Starting Position:
X1 starts with the ball and makes a pass to O5. O5 then kicks the ball to the goalkeeper. The goalkeeper throws the ball to X4 who makes a diagonal run to collect the ball. Switch the start point between X1/O5 and X2/O6.

Practice Sequence:
When O5 has kicked the ball to the goalkeeper the practice is live. The goalkeeper throws the ball to X4 who should have made a diagonal run to create enough space to receive the ball. All other X players should be making diagonal runs and prepared to receive the ball.

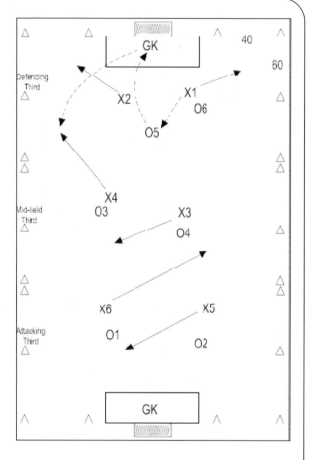

Running with the ball

General:
Set up a small sided game marked with cones at 60 X 40 yards with 2 full size goals and cones marking the different thirds of the playing field.

Use 12 players plus 2 goalkeepers and coach only one unit of 6 players and a goalkeeper at one time.

Specific:
All X players should create space so that the player with the ball is able to run into space. If not enough space can be created, re-position the defending players O5 or O6.

Skills for running with the ball

When to run with the ball:
A player should only run with the ball when there is space available and there is not a better alternative, such as passing to a player in a better position or crossing the ball early behind the defense.

How to run with the ball:
The ball should be played forward, enough to maintain a balanced stride.

When playing the ball forward the player should look up to asses the play and make a decision whether to run with the ball further or end the run.

When the player decides to end the run, the player should pass to another player, shoot or cross the ball behind the defense. In any case, this decision should be made before losing the advantage and being tackled by a defending player.

KEY

Ball Movement	⟶		Player Movement	⇢
Attacking Player	X		Defending Player	0
Server	S		Goalkeeper	GK

Key Factors:

1. Run with the ball when there is space available.
2. With the first touch, play the ball forward.
3. Look up between kicking the ball forward to asses the play.
4. Know when to end the run and what to do with the ball.

EQUIPMENT: Small sided field 60 x 40 yards 10 Balls, Bibs, Cones — TIME: 20 min.

Starting Position:

X2 starts with the ball and makes a pass to O5. O5 then kicks the ball to the goalkeeper. The goalkeeper throws the ball to X3.

Switch the start point between X2/O5 and X1/O6.

Practice Sequence:

When O5 has kicked the ball to the goalkeeper the practice is live.

The goalkeeper throws the ball to X3 who should have created enough space to receive the ball

All other X players should make space to allow X3 to run with the ball or pass to another player who is in a position to run with the ball.

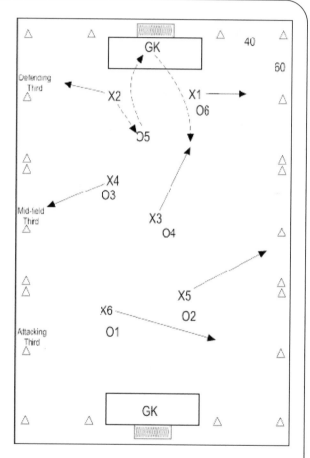

When and where to dribble

General:
Set up a small sided game marked with cones at 60 X 40 yards with 2 full size goals and cones marking the different thirds of the playing field.

Use 12 players plus 2 goalkeepers and coach only one unit of 6 players and a goalkeeper at one time.

Specific:
The players should not be restricted where they play on the field, only when and where the dribbling takes place.

Skills for when and where to dribble the ball

Defense:
Dribbling should be discouraged in the defensive third of the field. In this area encourage passing and creating space for each other to move the ball forward.

Mid-field:
Running with the ball should be encouraged, but dribbling only when necessary.

Attack:
In a one on one situation with a defender, encourage dribbling and attacking the space in front of the goal. Once a dribble is successful, encourage a shot on goal or a pass to an unmarked supporting player.

KEY			
Ball Movement	⟶	Player Movement	- - - - - ->
Attacking Player	X	Defending Player	0
Server	S	Goalkeeper	GK

Key Factors:

1. Run with the ball when there is space available.
2. With the first touch, play the ball forward.
3. Look up between kicking the ball forward to asses the play.
4. Know when to end the run and what to do with the ball.

EQUIPMENT: Small sided field 60 x 40 yards 10 Balls, Bibs, Cones   TIME: 20 min.

Starting Position:

X4 starts with the ball and passes to O5. O5 then passes the ball to X3.

Switch the start point between X4/O5/X3 and X3/O6/X4.

Practice Sequence:

When O5 has passed the ball to X3 the practice is live.

All other X players should make space to allow X3 to either dribble the ball or make a pass to another X player.

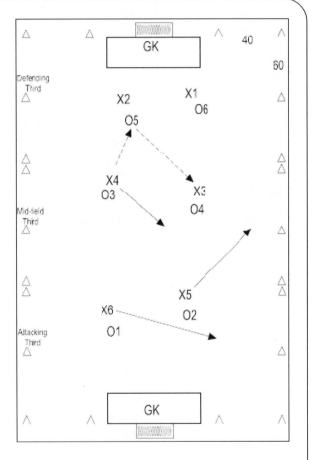

Shooting from a distance

General:
Set up a small sided game marked with cones at 60 X 40 yards with 2 full size goals, and cones marking the different thirds of the playing field.

Use 12 players plus 2 goalkeepers and coach only one unit of 6 players and a goalkeeper at one time.

Specific:
The practice should begin in the mid-field area to create shooting possibilities as soon as possible.

The defending players O1 and O2 should not leave the defending third. The attacking players X5 and X6 are the only X players allowed inside the attacking third.
X5 and X6 are not allowed to shoot inside the attacking third and must pass back to another player outside the attacking third.

Techniques and skills for shooting from a distance

Shooting from a distance:
To prevent overreaching, get well up to the ball and allow the body weight to be transferred to the shot.

The player should have an aggressive attitude towards striking the ball and be determined to score.

Accuracy is still more important than power, even at a great distance.

General:
The player should observe the movement and the position of the goalkeeper and the defending players.

The player should not shoot if one of the defenders can block the shot, but should pass the ball to another player in a better position.

KEY

Ball Movement	⟶		Player Movement	- - - - - - - →
Attacking Player	X		Defending Player	0
Server	S		Goalkeeper	GK

Key Factors:
1. Observe position and the movement of the goalkeeper.
2. Selection of shot.
3. Accuracy over power.
4. Get well up to the ball to avoid overreaching.

EQUIPMENT: SMALL SIDED FIELD 60 X 40 YARDS, 10 BALLS, BIBS, CONES

TIME: 20 MIN.

Starting Position:
X6 passes the ball to O3 who passes to X5 and the play is active. Alternate the starting position to X5/O4/X6 and X6/O3/X5.

Practice Sequence:
When O3 has passed the ball to X5 the practice is live.

All other X players should make space to allow X5 to either dribble the ball or make a pass to another X player.

O1/ O2 and X5/X6 are the only players allowed in the attacking third but X5/X6 must pass back out of the attacking third to shoot. All X players can shoot at any time but outside the attacking third.

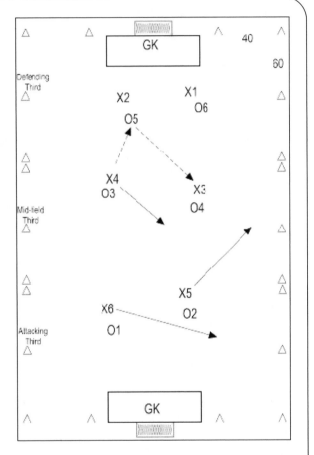

141

Attacking and shooting around the goal

General:
Set up a small sided game marked with cones at 60 X 40 yards with 2 full size goals, and cones marking the different thirds of the playing field.

Cones should be placed marking a V shaped grid for shooting, stretching from the goalposts to the outside cones marking the middle of the attacking third.

Use 12 players plus 2 goalkeepers and coach only one unit of 6 players and a goalkeeper at one time.

Specific:
The angle of the V shaped grid should be positioned so that shooting inside of the V is a high percentage shot, and shooting outside will be a low percentage shot. This will depend on the ability and age of the players.

Skills for attacking and shooting around the goal

When and where to Shoot:
Shoot within the V coned area in front of the goal, if a defender is not blocking the shooting possibility, and it is within range of the players' ability.

When and where not to shoot:
When an opponent is so close as to be certain to block the shot.

When the distance is so great that it gives an unacceptable percentage chance of missing the target.

If the angle is so small that it gives an unacceptable chance of scoring a goal, then the ball should be passed to another player who has a better opportunity to shoot.

KEY

Ball Movement	→	Player Movement	----→
Attacking Player	X	Defending Player	0
Server	S	Goalkeeper	GK

Key Factors:
1. Observe the position and the movement of the goalkeeper.
2. Shoot from inside the V grid only.
3. Pass or cross from outside the V grid.
4. Selection and accuracy of the shot.

EQUIPMENT: SMALL SIDED FIELD 60 x 40 YARDS, 10 BALLS, BIBS, CONES   **TIME: 20** MIN.

Starting Position:
X3 starts with the ball and makes a pass to O4. O4 then passes to X4. Switch the start point between X3/O4/X4 and X4/O3/X3.

Practice Sequence:
When O4 has passed the ball to X4 the practice is live.
Both X5 and X6 must create enough space to receive the ball. Only O1 and O2 are allowed inside the attacking third, but the four X players X3, X4, X5 and X6 are allowed inside the attacking third.

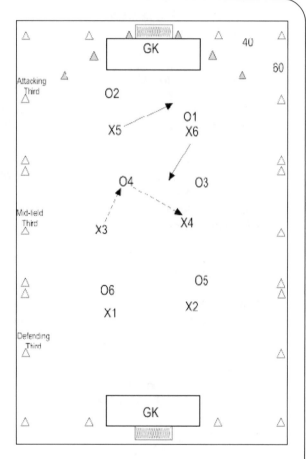

143

Defending in an attacking position

General:
Set up a small sided game marked with cones at 60 X 40 yards with 2 full size goals.

Use 12 players plus 2 goalkeepers and coach only one unit of 6 players and a goalkeeper at one time.

Specific:
Coach the X players to defend in an attacking position.

If the X players defend too quickly or before the O player receives the ball, make one of the X players defend against the goalkeeper first, before defending against the O player.

Skills for defending in attack

Defending:
The defending player should watch the ball when in a challenging position.

It is important for the defending player to adopt the ideal position which is a little less than 1 to 1.5 yards from the attacker.

The defender should be patient and concentrate on when to select the correct moment to tackle. The best moment is when the attacker attempts to turn.

Supporting:
The supporting player should be positioned at an angle behind the defender, in line with where the attacker is being steered.

The supporting player should communicate with the defender.

KEY

Ball Movement	⟶		Player Movement	⟶
Attacking Player	X		Defending Player	0
Server	S		Goalkeeper	GK

Key Factors:
1. Close the space down quickly between defender and attacker
2. Angle and speed of the defending players run.
3. Players position to prevent the ball being played forward.
3. Supporting players position and communication.

EQUIPMENT: Small sided field 60 x 40 yards, 10 Balls, Bibs, Cones   **TIME:** 20 min.

Starting Position:

X1 starts with the ball and makes a pass to O6. O6 then kicks the ball to the goalkeeper.
The goalkeeper can pass to either X1 or X2.
Switch the start point between X1/O6 and X2/O5.

Practice Sequence:

When O6 has kicked the ball to the goalkeeper the practice is live. Both X1 and X2 must create enough space to receive the ball. The O players must defend to regain possession of the ball quickly.

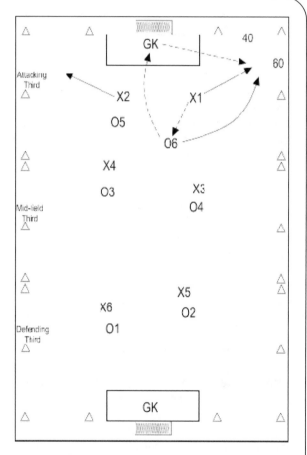

Defensive recovery

General:
Set up a small sided game marked with cones at 60 X 40 yards with 2 full size goals, and cones marking the different thirds of the playing field.

Set out cones marking the V shape recovery area from the goal posts to the halfway line.

Use 12 players plus 2 goalkeepers and coach only one unit of 6 players and a goalkeeper at one time.

Specific:
The O players must recover quickly when the X players are in possession of the ball and create a good shape to defend their goal.

Skills for defensive recovery

When do you need to recover?:
A player should recover to support the defense when the opposition has regained possession of the ball and the defenders goal side of the ball are outnumbered.

How do you recover?:
The player should run as quickly as possible, taking the shortest route into the V shape defensive area.

Where to recover to:
When the player has reached a position behind the ball, the player should either challenge the opponent with the ball or support the defender challenging the opponent with ball.

If players are already defending against the opponent with the ball, then they should mark another opponent or occupy important space goal side of the ball.

KEY

Ball Movement	⟶	Player Movement	--------➤
Attacking Player	X	Defending Player	0
Server	S	Goalkeeper	GK

Key Factors:
1. Retreat, taking the shortest route to support the defense.
2. Recover inside a V shape area.
3. Recover to a position behind the ball and deny space to the attackers.
4. Player communications.

EQUIPMENT: Small sided field 60 x 40 yards, V grid, 10 Balls, Bibs, Cones

TIME: 20 min.

Starting Position:
X2 starts with the ball and makes a pass to O5. O5 then kicks the ball back to the goalkeeper.
The goalkeeper kicks the ball down the field to one of the X players.
Switch the start point between X2/O5 and X1/O6.

Practice Sequence:
When O5 has kicked the ball back to the goalkeeper the practice is live.
The X players must create enough space to receive the ball.
The players have no restrictions and can play in any part of the field.

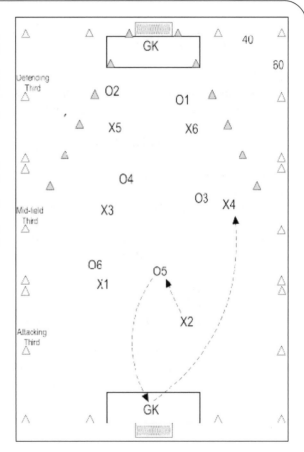

Attacking with crosses

General:
Set up a small sided game marked with cones at 60 X 40 yards with 2 full size goals, and cones marking the different thirds of the playing field.

The running lanes should be 10 X 60 yards on each side of the small sided playing field.

Use 12 players plus 2 goalkeepers and coach only one unit of 6 players and a goalkeeper at one time.

Specific:
The ball can be played at any time to one of the crossing players, but a goal cannot be scored unless a crossing player has made a cross.

Skills for attacking with crosses

Players crossing the ball:
The crossing player should make a run with the ball in the crossing lane and before the end of the lane make a lofted pass behind the defense.

The cross should be played accurately behind the defense, selecting the area where the attackers can attack the ball.

Attacking players:
The attacking players should wait and see where the ball is going to land, and at the correct time make an angled run to the oncoming ball.

The attacking players should be first to the ball and make the decision to play directly to the goal, across to the other side of the goal, or play the ball back to another player.

		KEY		
Ball Movement	⟶	Player Movement	---------➤	
Attacking Player	X	Defending Player	0	
Server	S	Goalkeeper	GK	

Key Factors:

1. Cross the ball early behind the defense.
2. Attackers should observe the position of the defense and the goalkeeper.
3. The attacker's angle and timing of the run.
4. Attackers should be first to the ball.

EQUIPMENT: SMALL SIDED FIELD 60 x 40 YARDS, RUNNING LANES, 10 BALLS, BIBS, CONES

TIME: 20 MIN.

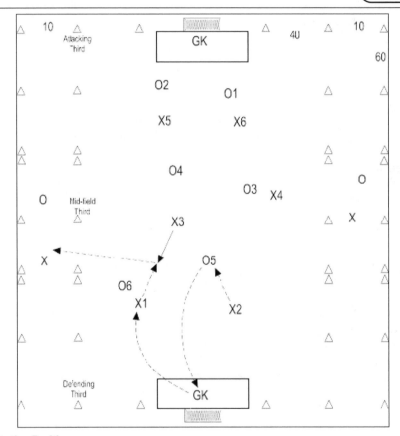

Starting Position:

X2 starts with the ball and makes a pass to O5. O5 then kicks the ball back to the goalkeeper. The goalkeeper throws the ball to X1 who passes to the oncoming X3. X3 should make a pass to the crossing player in the crossing lane.

Switch the start point between X2/O5 /X1 and X1/O6/X2.

Practice Sequence:

When O5 has kicked the ball back to the goalkeeper the practice is live.

The X players must use the crossing players and cannot score a goal unless the ball has first been played to a crossing player in the same practice sequence.

Only the crossing players are allowed inside the crossing lanes.

Defending players and space

General:
Set up a small sided game marked with cones of 60 X 40 yards with 2 full size goals, and cones marking the different thirds of the playing field.

Use 12 players plus 2 goalkeepers and coach only one unit of 6 players and a goalkeeper at one time.

Specific:
If, at the start, X3 or X4 are defended quickly by O3 or O4, move O3 or O4 further away to give more time for the X players to control the ball.

Skills for defending players and space

Defending:
The defending player should always keep goal side of the opponent and occupy space.

The defender should always keep the opponent and the ball in view.

The defender should be close enough to challenge the opponent when the ball is passed to the opponent.

The defender should force the opponent to defensive strength and/or out of the grid area.

Supporting:
The supporting player should be positioned at an angle behind the defender, in line with where the attacker is being steered.

The supporting player should communicate with the defender.

KEY

Ball Movement	⟶		Player Movement	------→
Attacking Player	X		Defending Player	O
Server	S		Goalkeeper	GK

Key Factors:

1. Close the space down quickly between defender and attacker.
2. Angle and speed of the defending player's run.
3. Players' position to prevent the ball from being played forward.
4. Supporting players' position and communication.

EQUIPMENT: SMALL SIDED FIELD 60 x 40 CREATED WITH CONES, DIVIDED INTO THIRDS, 10 BALLS, BIBS

TIME: 20 MIN.

Starting Position:

X4 passes to O4 who passes to X3. When the ball is played to X3 the practice is live.

Alternate between X4/O4/X3 and X3/O3/X4.

Practice Sequence:

Coach the O players.

As soon as the practice is live all O defenders should be either defending a player or space but within distance of an unmarked opponent.

Practice using both the left and right sides of the playing field.

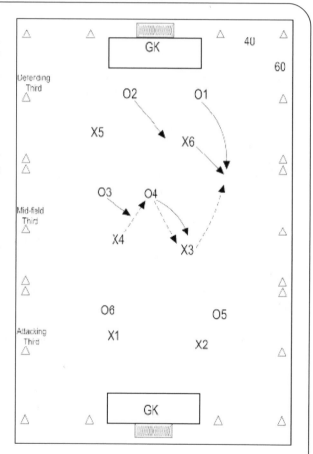

Creating width and length

General:
Set up a small sided game marked with cones at 60 X 40 yards with 2 full size goals, and cones marking the different thirds of the playing field.

Use 12 players plus 2 goalkeepers and coach only one unit of 6 players and a goalkeeper at one time.

Specific:
The practice should start with one of the 2 defenders on either side of the goal.

As soon as the goalkeeper has control of the ball, the X team should react to create the necessary width and length.

Skills for creating width and length

Passing:
The pace of the ball must be with enough pace to reach its target but not so strong that it is difficult to control.

The timing of the pass should maximize the position of the player receiving the pass and place the opponents at a disadvantage.

Running:
The player should make a controlled run, always expecting the ball to be passed.

Run behind the defense or wide to create space to receive the ball.

KEY

Ball Movement	⟶	Player Movement	------⟶
Attacking Player	X	Defending Player	0
Server	S	Goalkeeper	GK

Key Factors:

1. Team with possession run wide and be ready to receive the ball.
2. Attackers run deep to draw the opposing defenders and create space.
3. Mid-field players run wide or deep depending on the space available.
4. All players run quickly and keep an eye on the player with the ball.

EQUIPMENT: SMALL SIDED FIELD 60 x 40 CREATED WITH CONES, DIVIDED INTO THIRDS, 10 BALLS, BIBS

TIME: 20 MIN.

Starting Position:

X2 passes to O6 who makes a lofted pass to the goalkeeper.
The goalkeeper throws the ball to X1 and the play is live.
Alternate between X2/O6 and X1/O5 to start the sequence.

Practice Sequence:

Coach the X players.

All the players should create space from their respective defending players and be ready to receive the ball.

The defenders should run wide and be ready to receive the ball.

The mid-field players should create space from their defenders and be ready to receive the ball.

The attacking players should create space to receive a long forward pass.

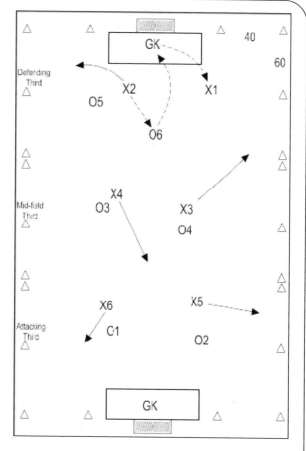

Forward passing

General:
Set up a small sided game marked with cones at 60 X 40 yards with 2 full size goals, and cones marking the different thirds of the playing field.

Use 12 players plus 2 goalkeepers and coach only one unit of 6 players and a goalkeeper at one time.

Specific:
When the goalkeeper has control of the ball either X1 or X2 should be ready to receive the ball, depending on which defender was used to start the sequence.

If the attackers X1 or X2 are closed down too quickly, ask the O player who kicked the ball to the goalkeeper to defend against the goalkeeper first.

Techniques and skills for forward passing

Body position:
The body should be open with the player able to the see the whole playing area.

The ball should be controlled with the outside foot and the head should come up to view the passing options.

Passing check list:
a. Pass into the back of the defense.
b. Next best forward pass.
c. Run forward with the ball to get a better position.
d. Switch the play inside to the mid-field.
e. Pass back to the defense or the goalkeeper.

	KEY		
Ball Movement	⟶	Player Movement	- - - - - - - ⟶
Attacking Player	X	Defending Player	0
Server	S	Goalkeeper	GK

Key Factors:

1. Control the ball with the first touch using the outside foot.
2. Keep an open body stance and view the playing situation.
3. Select passing option.
4. All players create space to receive the ball from a forward pass.

EQUIPMENT: SMALL SIDED FIELD 60 x 40 CREATED WITH CONES, DIVIDED INTO THIRDS, 10 BALLS, BIBS

TIME: 20 MIN.

Starting Position:

For left side practice, X2 passes to O6 who passes to the goalkeeper and the goalkeeper throws the ball to X1.

For right side practice, X1 passes to O5 who passes to the goalkeeper and the goalkeeper throws the ball to X2

Practice Sequence:

Coach the X players.

The goalkeeper should only throw the ball to either X1 or X2.

X1 or X2 should create space to receive the ball while other players create space to receive the forward pass.

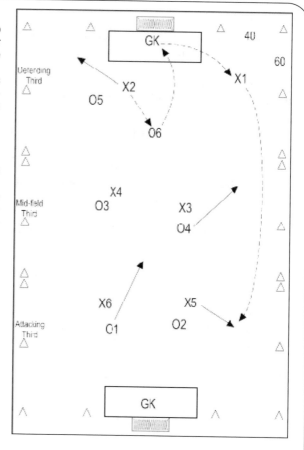

155

Keeping team possession of the ball

General:
Set up a small sided game marked with cones at 60 X 40 yards with 2 full size goals, and cones marking the different thirds of the playing field.

Use 12 players plus 2 goalkeepers and coach only one unit of 6 players and a goalkeeper at one time.

Specific:
The pass from the goalkeeper should be to one of the X players in the defensive third of the field.

If the defenders are closed down too quickly, make one of the O players in the defending third mark the goalkeeper.

Skills for ball possession

Passing to keep ball possession:
The pass should be accurate and the timing should be to maximize the position of the receiving player.

A variety of techniques should be used depending on the position of the receiving player.

The passing player should try to disguise where the pass is going.

Support:
The supporting player should arrive at the correct position at the right time to receive the ball and be prepared to control the ball in a crowded area.

Always be ready to receive a pass from another team player and get quickly into position.

	KEY		
Ball Movement	⟶	Player Movement	- - - - ▸
Attacking Player	X	Defending Player	0
Server	S	Goalkeeper	GK

Key Factors:
1. Close control of the ball.
2. Shield the ball while looking for a teammate.
3. Create space to receive the ball while not in possession of the ball.
4. Team communicates with each other and always ready to receive the ball.

EQUIPMENT: SMALL SIDED FIELD 60 x 40 CREATED WITH CONES, DIVIDED INTO THIRDS, 10 BALLS, BIBS

TIME: 20 MIN.

Starting Position:
X1 passes to O5 who makes a lofted pass to the goalkeeper. The goalkeeper throws the ball to either X1 or X2.
Alternate between X1/O5 and X2/O6 to start the sequence.

Practice Sequence:
Coach the X players.
The players should keep to their specific third of the field but the player making a successful pass into the next third can join that third of the field while his team is in possession of the ball.
This would mean if X2 makes a pass to X4 then X2 can run into the mid-field third and continue playing.
If the X team lose possession of the ball then all X players must return to their original third.

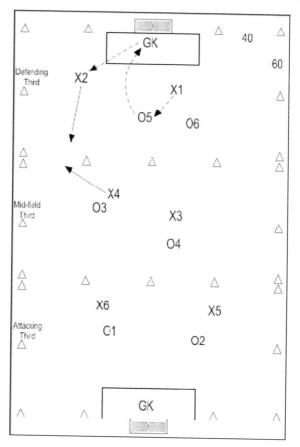

Creating shooting opportunities

General:
Set up a small sided game marked with cones at 60 X 40 yards with 2 full size goals, and cones marking the different thirds of the playing field.

Use 12 players plus 2 goalkeepers and coach only one unit of 6 players and a goalkeeper at one time.

Specific:
If at the start X3 or X4 are defended too quickly by O3 or O4, make O3 or O4 play further away to give more time for the X players to control the ball.

Do not allow the mid-field defenders O3 and O4 into the attacking third, but one of the attacking mid-fielders can run into the attacking third to support or shoot.

Skills for creating shooting opportunities

Attitude:
The players must take responsibility and shoot wherever and whenever possible.

Missing the target should not deter the player from shooting again, as missing an opportunity to shoot is worse than missing the target.

Shoot determined to score a goal.

Shooting:
Accuracy is more important than power even over a great distance.

The shot should be within the range of the players' ability.

Check the position of the goalkeeper and the opponents before shooting.

Do not shoot if an opponent can block the shot but pass to a player who has a better opportunity to shoot.

KEY

Ball Movement	→	Player Movement	---->
Attacking Player	X	Defending Player	0
Server	S	Goalkeeper	GK

Key Factors:

1. Check the position of the defense and the goalkeeper.
2. Accuracy over power.
3. Shoot at first opportunity if within range and not blocked by an opponent.
4. If it is not possible to shoot, pass to a player with a better opportunity.

EQUIPMENT: SMALL SIDED FIELD 60 x 40 CREATED WITH CONES, DIVIDED INTO THIRDS, 10 BALLS, BIBS

TIME: 20 MIN.

Starting Position:

X3 passes to O3 who passes to X4.

X4 should make a forward pass to either X6, X5 or X3.

Alternate starting between X3/O3/X4 and X4/O4/X3.

Practice Sequence:

Coach the X players.

X5 and X6 should only play in the attacking third with O1 and O2.

X3 and X4 should only play in the mid-field third with O3 and O4.

X1 and X2 should only play in the defending third with O5 and O6.

While the X team is in possession of the ball either X3 or X4 can join the attacking third of the field.

For example X3 can play in the attacking third while X4, X5 or X6 is in possession of the ball.

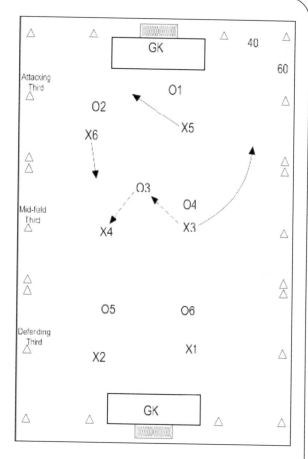

PHASES OF PLAY: PRACTICE DESCRIPTION

Three man defense with a sweeper

General:
For this phase of play, use 6 defenders plus a sweeper and goalkeeper against 7 attackers and coach the defense.

Create 2 goals on the half way line of about 5 yards wide and 10 yards from the side line.

Specific:
The server is the starting position but the ball is in play when the first player receives the ball.

The O players can score a goal in either of the 2 small goals on the half way line.

Skills for defending with a sweeper

Sweeper positioning:
Always keep goal side of the opponent and occupy space, moving around the penalty spot behind or ahead of the defense.

Keep all opponents and the ball in view, especially on the blind side of the field.

Sweeper Responsibilities:
Mark the unmarked player inside or outside shooting distance.

Defend against an unmarked player with the ball attacking the goal or making a pass into the penalty area.

Positioning and communicating with the team when the ball is being played outside the penalty area.

KEY

Ball Movement	⟶	Player Movement	------>
Attacking Player	X	Defending Player	0
Server	S	Goalkeeper	GK

Key Factors:

1. Sweeper position around the penalty spot.
2. Communicating with the defense.
3. Keep the ball and all players in view.
4. Defend the unmarked player.

EQUIPMENT: SMALL SIDED FIELD 60 x 40 CREATED WITH CONES, DIVIDED INTO THIRDS, 10 BALLS, BIBS

TIME: 20 MIN.

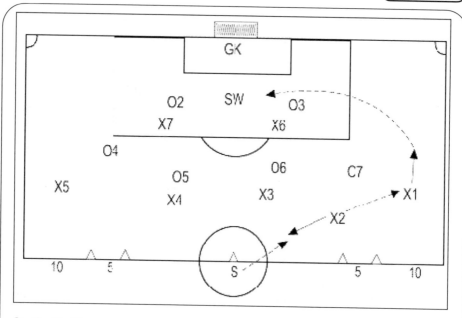

Starting Position:

The server plays the ball to one of the mid-field X players X2,X3,X4 and the practice is live.
The mid-field player should pass the ball to the wing players either X1 or X5.

Practice Sequence:

Coach the O players.

The midfield players should try to pass the ball to one of the wing players X1 or X5 and they should make a cross into the penalty area.

The mid-field players should try to pass the ball across the field where possible.

The defending O players should defend against the X players realistically.

The sequence should start with the sweeper at a central point around the penalty spot. Once the sequence has started the sweeper can move as necessary.

Passing and making diagonal runs

General:
For this phase of play, use 8 defenders plus a goalkeeper and coach the 8 attackers.

Create 2 goals on the half way line of about 5 yards wide and 10 yards from the side line.

Specific:
The server is the starting position but the ball is in play when the first player receives the ball.

The O players can score a goal in either of the 2 small goals on the half way line.

Skills for passing and making diagonal runs

Running:
The players should make diagonal runs into space where the ball could be played, and be prepared to receive the ball.

Passing:
The pass should be accurate and the timing should be to maximize the position of the receiving player.

A variety of techniques should be used depending on the position of the receiving player.

The passing player should try to disguise where the pass is going.

	KEY		
Ball Movement	⟶	Player Movement	⇢
Attacking Player	X	Defending Player	0
Server	S	Goalkeeper	GK

Key Factors :
1. Timing and accuracy of the passes and pace on the ball.
2. Timing and angle of the runs.
3. Runs should be diagonal across the field.
4. Run quickly but at a controlled speed.

EQUIPMENT: HALF A SOCCER FIELD WITH THE GOAL AND PENALTY AREA, BALLS, BIBS, CONES

TIME: 20 MIN.

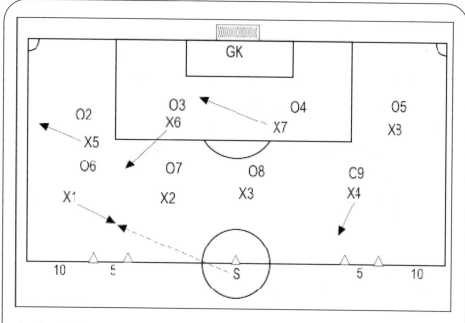

Starting Position:
The 2 outside mid-field players X1 and X4 should create space to receive the ball from the server.
The server plays the ball to one of the outside mid-field X1 or X4 and the practice is live.

Practice Sequence:
Coach the X players.
The outside midfield player should try to pass the ball to another X player who should create space by making a diagonal run.
The O players should defend against the X players realistically.

Crossing and finishing

General:
For this phase of play use 7 defenders plus a goalkeeper and coach the 8 attackers.

Create 2 goals on the half way line of about 5 yards wide and 10 yards from the side line.

Specific:
At the start of the sequence bring the players out of the penalty area to make space.

When the first player has received the ball from the server, play is active.

The O players can score a goal in either of the 2 small goals on the half way line.

Techniques and skills for crossing and finishing

Crossing the ball:
The crossing player should make a controlled run with the ball, kicking the ball with the outside of the foot.

Between kicking the ball, the crossing player should keep the head up to assess the position of the players.

The cross can be a ground pass or a lofted pass to the near or far post.

Finishing from crosses:
The attacking players should make an angled run so as to be facing the ball when it is delivered.

The time to attack is when the crossing players' head goes down to cross the ball.

The attacking player should take the first opportunity to get in front of the defense and play the ball first time.

KEY

Ball Movement	⟶	Player Movement	------>
Attacking Player	X	Defending Player	0
Server	S	Goalkeeper	GK

Key Factors:

1. Run at controlled speed with the ball under control.
2. Cross the ball using a ground, chip or lofted pass.
3. Create space away from the opponent by moving the opposite direction to the ball.
4. Time to move is when the crossing players' head goes down to cross the ball.

EQUIPMENT: HALF A SOCCER FIELD WITH THE GOAL AND PENALTY AREA, BALLS, BIBS, CONES

TIME: 20 MIN.

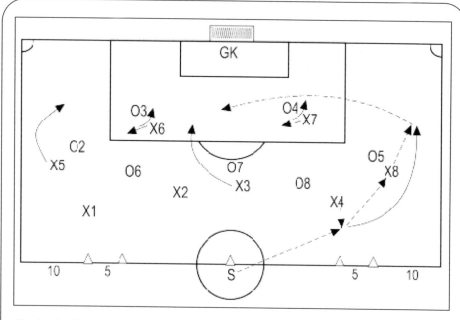

Starting Position:

Move all players out of the penalty area.

The server plays the ball to X4 and the practice is live.

X4 controls the ball and passes to X8, makes an overlap run to receive the return pass, and crosses the ball into the penalty area.

Alternate the start between X4/X8 on the right to X1/X5 on the left.

Practice Sequence:

Coach the X players.

The midfield player X4 runs to collect the ball from the server, passes to the outside mid-field player X8 and makes an overlap run. The return pass should be in the path of X4 and then X4 should make a cross into the penalty area.

The attackers should be prepared to receive the ball and make a good attempt to score a goal.

The central mid-field players should also be prepared to make an angled run into the area to score when possible.

The O defending players should defend against the X players realistically.

When and where to shoot

General:
For this phase of play use 6 defending players plus a goalkeeper and coach the 7 attackers.

Set up cones on the side line making sure they are in line with the penalty area, and at the side of the goal. Set up further cones on the penalty area in line with the cones by the goal and the side line.
Keep the number of cones to a minimum to create the V shaped area.
The angle of the V shape should ensure that shooting outside the area is not a good shooting angle for the players involved.
This can depend on the age and players' ability and may have to be adjusted accordingly.

Create 2 goals on the half way line of about 5 yards wide and 10 yards from the side line

Specific:
Either X3 or X4 is the starting position and the ball is in play when the first attacking player receives the ball.

The O players can score a goal in either of the 2 small goals on the half way line.

Skills for when and where to shoot

Where to shoot:
Shoot inside the V area in front of the goal, within the range of the player's ability, if a defender is not blocking the shooting possibility.

When to shoot:
When an opportunity arises and the opponents are outside the distance to block the shot.

When the distance to goal is such that it gives an acceptable percentage chance of hitting the target with pace and accuracy.

KEY

Ball Movement	⟶	Player Movement	- - - - - ⟶
Attacking Player	X	Defending Player	0
Server	S	Goalkeeper	GK

Key Factors:

1. Shoot inside the V area to give the best scoring opportunity.
2. Shoot within the range of the players' ability.
3. Do not shoot if an opponent can block the shot.
4. Dribble, pass or cross the ball from outside the shooting area.

EQUIPMENT: HALF A SOCCER FIELD WITH THE GOAL AND PENALTY AREA, BALLS, BIBS, CONES

TIME: 20 MIN.

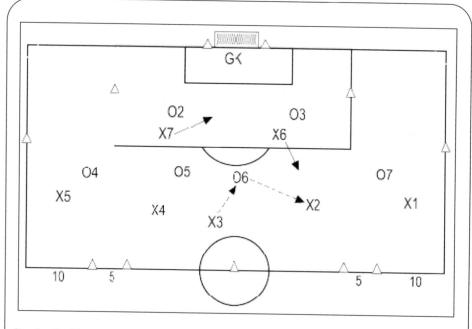

Starting Position:

X3 plays the ball to O6 who passes to X2 and the practice is live.
Alternate the start between X3/O6/X2 and X3/O5/X4.

Practice Sequence:

Coach the X players.
Set up the players so that the attacking team X has a numerical advantage over the defending team O.
When the ball is played from O6 to X2 all the X players should create space from their respective defending players to receive the ball.
The O defending players should defend against the X players realistically.

Goalkeeper communication and positioning

General:
For this phase of play use 6 attackers and coach the goalkeeper and the 6 defending players.

Create 2 goals on the half way line of about 5 yards wide and 10 yards from the side line.

Specific:
The server is the starting position but the ball is in play only when the first player receives the ball.

Skills for goalkeeper communication and position

Goalkeeper Communication:
Keep players informed of when and which opponents are not marked.

Communicate with the players with short understandable commands.

Goalkeeper positioning:
Keep all opponents and the ball in view, especially on the blind side, and move with the play to halve the distance to the last defender.

Be in line with the center of the goal but move further towards the far post of the goal when the opponents are in a crossing position.

KEY

Ball Movement	⟶	Player Movement	------→
Attacking Player	X	Defending Player	0
Server	S	Goalkeeper	GK

Key Factors:

1. Affect team positions on the field.
2. Recovery communications.
3. Communicate blind side information.
4. Goalkeeper positioned half the distance from the last defender.

EQUIPMENT: HALF A SOCCER FIELD WITH THE GOAL AND PENALTY AREA, BALLS, BIBS, CONES

TIME: 20 MIN.

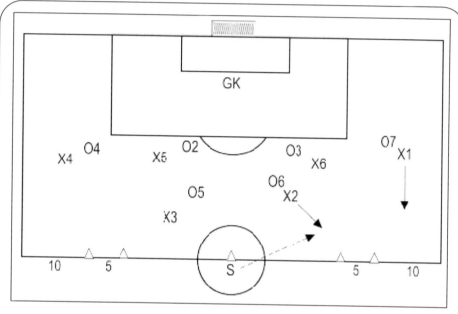

Starting Position:

All the O players should move out of the penalty area and the goalkeeper should be on the goal area line. The server plays the ball to either X2 or X3 and the practice is live.

Practice Sequence:

Coach the goalkeeper and the O players.
The goalkeeper should have a central point to start and move when necessary.
The goalkeeper should communicate defenders' positioning.
The X players should create space from their respective defending players to receive the ball.
The defending O players should defend against the X players realistically.
The O players can score a goal in either of the 2 small goals on the half way line.

NOTES

SECTION IV: PRACTICE INDEX

Goalkeeping:

NOTES

Section V: Coaches Corner

General Practice Sessions

In a general practice it is possible to train with 2 themes in mind, however it is useful to keep the themes similar so that the practice sessions do not have too many key factors.

The following is a suggestion for a 24 practice session schedule and is an example of how you can prepare a total training schedule utilizing this book. However, with a little imagination many variations can be achieved.

24 Sample practice sessions

Practice 1 passing and running
Ground passes	session 1
Creating space with over lap running	session 32
Diagonal running	session 63

Practice 2 ball control and passing
Individual Running with Ball Control	session 18
Ground passing accuracy	session 21
Keeping Team Possession of the ball	session 74

Practice 3 distance passing and creating space
Lofted passes	session 2
Attacking by crossing the ball	session 40
Creating space	session 61

Practice 4 creating space and shooting
Turning and creating space to shoot	session 28
Running at angles	session 51
When and where to shoot	session 79

Practice 5 shooting
Basic shooting	session 7
Active shooting	session 34
Attacking and shooting around the goal	session 67

Practice 6 defending and counter attacking
Ball handling in an attacking position	session 26
Defending players and space	session 71
Forward passing	session 73

Coaches Corner

Practice 7 ball control and defending

Ball control while running — session 5
Defending as a team — session 38
Defending in an attacking position — session 68

Practice 8 crossing and attacking

Attacking in front of the goal — session 29
Crossing from the side of the penalty area — session 55
Crossing and finishing — session 78

Practice 9 dribbling and attacking

Dribbling techniques — session 17
Dribbling in attack — session 59
Attacking inside the penalty area — session 56

Practice 10 dribbling and attacking

Dribbling — session 4
Attacking in and around the penalty area — session 42
Running with the ball — session 64

Practice 11 passing and creating space

Creating space as an individual — session 12
Passing as a group — session 31
Creating space — session 61

Practice 12 passing and creating space

One touch practice — session 19
Creating space by passing inside — session 47
Passing and making diagonal runs — session 77

Practice 13 goalkeeping and defending

Defending turning and support — session 9
Passing back to the goalkeeper — session 43
Defending the penalty area — session 37

Practice 14 goalkeeping and defending

Goalkeeping shots — session 30
Defending against opponents facing the goal — session 48
Goalkeeper distributing by throwing the ball — session 60

Practice 15 shooting and attacking
Shooting across the goal	session 8
One on one with the goalkeeper	session 36
Attacking with crosses	session 70

Practice 16 attacking and shooting
Running and shooting	session 27
Creating space in attack	session 53
Attacking across the penalty area	session 57

Practice 17 defending and passing
Defending turning and support	session 9
Defending around the penalty area	session 10
Overlap running	session 62

Practice 18 defending and passing
Passing and running	session 20
Defending by marking players	session 24
Defending and supporting in the penalty area	session 49

Practice 19 ball control and attacking
Trapping the ball	session 3
Attacking the ball around the goal	session 41
Diagonal running	session 63

Practice 20 ball control and attacking
Running with the ball	session 23
Running and passing at close angles	session 58
Creating width and length	session 72

Practice 21 creating goal opportunities and shooting
When and when not to shoot	session 35
Diagonal passing and running in attack	session 39
Shooting from a distance	session 66

Practice 22 creating goal opportunities
Lofted forward passing	session 22
Finishing from crosses	session 52
Creating shooting opportunities	session 75

COACHES CORNER

Practice 23 defending as a team
Tracking and marking players   session 11
Defending as a team   session 38
Defensive recovery   session 69

Practice 24 defending as a team
Prevent opponents from turning   session 25
Defending with a sweeper   session 50
Three man defense with a sweeper   session 76

COACHES CORNER

Example themes with sessions combinations

Passing:

Ground passes	session 1
Passing as a group	session 31
Diagonal running	session 63

Passing:

Ground passing accuracy	session 21
Passing and running	session 20
Running and passing at close angles	session 58

Passing as a team:

Lofted forward passing	session 22
Forward passing	session 73
Passing and making diagonal runs	session 77

Ball control:

Dribbling	session 4
Heading the ball	session 6
When and where to dribble	session 65

Ball control:

Dribbling techniques	session 17
Running with the ball	session 23
Keeping Team Possession of the ball	session 74

Creating space:

Ball control while running	session 5
Creating space with wall passing	session 33
Creating space	session 61

Creating space:

One touch practice	session 19
Creating space by passing inside	session 47
Creating width and length	session 72

Shooting:

Running and shooting	session 27
Finishing from crosses	session 52
Creating shooting opportunities	session 75

COACHES CORNER

Shooting accuracy:

Shooting attitude:

Marking and defending:

Marking and defending:

Defending as a team:

Defending as a team:

Goalkeeping with the team:

Creating goal opportunities:

COACHES CORNER

Creating goal opportunities:

Running and crossing the ball	session 13
Attacking in and around the penalty area	session 42
Attacking with crosses	session 70

Crossing:

Attacking in front of the goal	session 29
Crossing from the end line	session 54
Crossing and finishing	session 78

TITLE:

Key Factors:
1.
2.
3.
4.

EQUIPMENT:

TIME: MIN.

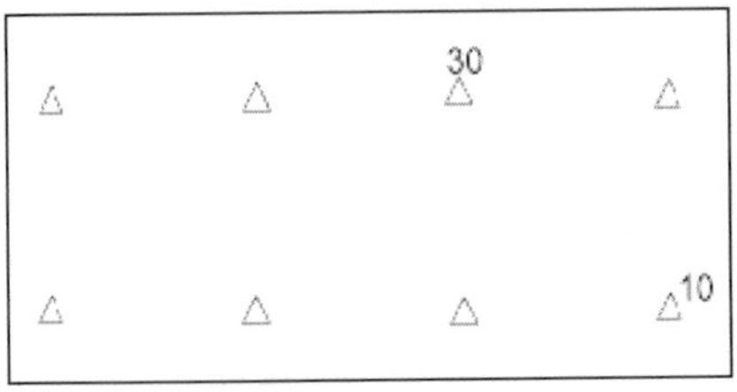

Practice Sequence 1

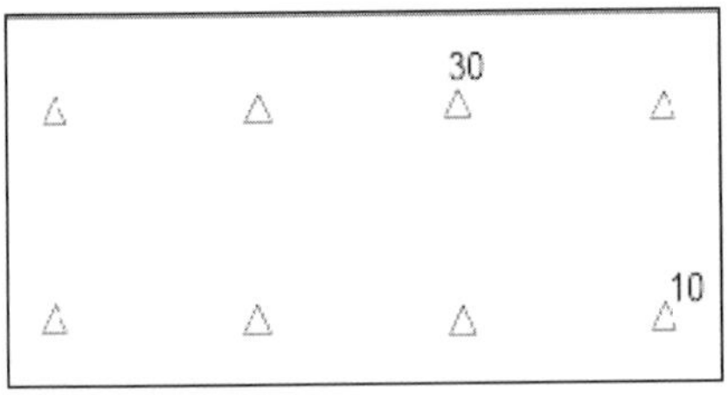

Practice Sequence 2

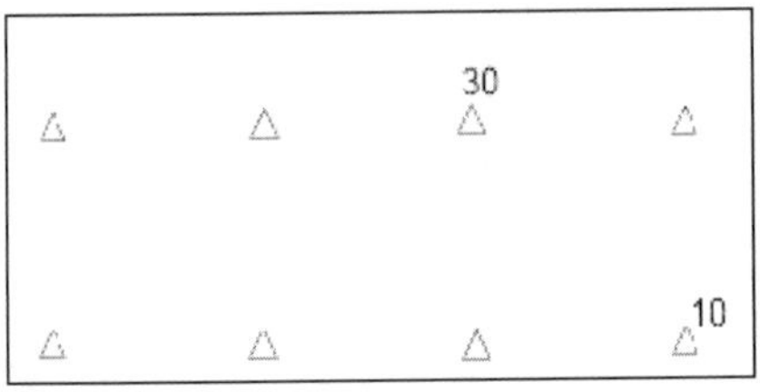

Practice Sequence 3

TITLE: (NO.)

Key Factors:
1.
2.
3.
4.

EQUIPMENT: GOAL AND PENALTY AREA (**TIME:** MIN.)

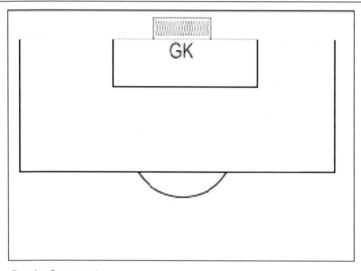

Practice Sequence 1

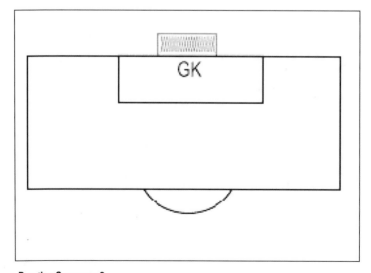

Practice Sequence 2

Key Factors:

1.
2.
3.
4.

EQUIPMENT: SMALL SIDED FIELD 60 x 40, 10 BALLS, BIBS

TIME   MIN.

Starting Position:

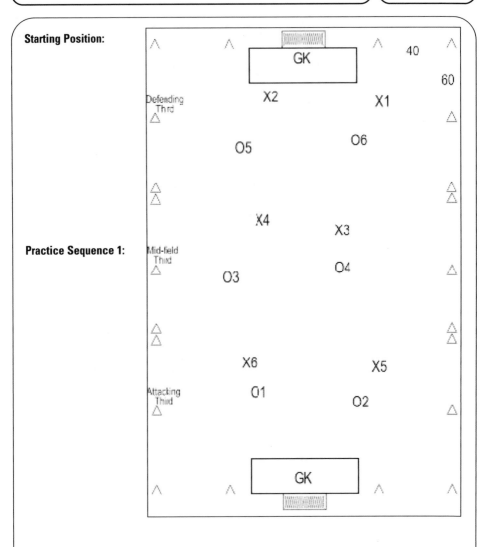

Practice Sequence 1:

Welcome to Soccer Soul where YOUR Soccer Coaching Information is free and just a click away.

www.soccersoul.com
www.soccersoul.co.uk

Create your own soccer coaching plan quickly, using the most up-to-date information from a wide variety of proven sources, utilizing Training Sessions from Soccer Soul.

Techniques and Skills offers you the choice to select and review different topics. These topics can be easily introduced into your practice sessions.

Themes and Analysis will help you to analyze how your team is performing. You can select different themes for your training program using Soccer Soul's Analysis Sheets.

Fitness and Diet will give you on-going information on fitness training sessions and different training diets.

Coaches' Forum allows you to contact other coaches and review articles on a wide range of subjects including first Aid and Injury information.

REEDSWAIN BOOKS

**#149 Soccer Tactics
An Analysis of Attack
and Defense**
by Massimo Lucchesi
$12.95

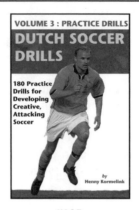

**#195
Dutch Soccer Drills
Vol. 3**
by Henny Kormelink
$12.95

**#249
Coaching the 3-4-3**
by Massimo Lucchesi
$12.95

**#188 300 Innovative
SOCCER Drills for
Total PLAYER
Development**
*by Roger Wilkinson
and Mick Critchell*
$14.95

**#185
Conditioning for Soccer**
by Dr. Raymond Verheijen
$19.95

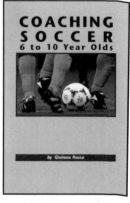

**#264 Coaching
Soccer
6 to 10 Year Olds**
by Giuliano Rusca
$14.95

1-800-331-5191 • WWW.REEDSWAIN.COM